California

MW01292900

The air is dry, suffocating, almost unbreathable – and not just because of the drought and the increasingly cataclysmic fires. This oppressive climate extends into the social sphere as well, and the California Dream is starting to look more like a dystopia. The list of paradoxes is striking: an ever-growing economy that prices people out of the state; a natural paradise that is now home to the six most polluted cities in the USA; students attending one of the world's most prestigious universities forced to live in tents because they can't afford to rent; an agricultural sector pursuing an unsustainable model of high-water-use crops in a drought-afflicted state ... That this (former?) promised land is seen as a breeding ground for future worldwide trends is both disturbing (are we heading in the same direction?) but also reassuring, because in California the wind of change never stops, and it blows in fresh air and excitement – particularly when it comes to the cultural sphere. Examples are everywhere: a new generation of Asian-American writers is rebelling against the stereotype of a uniform "model minority" – docile and hard-working – which has always been a doubling up of racist stereotyping, implying simultaneously that African Americans are "guilty" of not achieving similar levels of success. The Black communities, in their turn, are fighting against the gentrification and "whitening" of cities such as San Francisco and Los Angeles. In an era of historical reassessment, full of symbolic gestures – not least the "rematriation" of land to Indigenous people – there is no longer room for the colonial founding myths. It is time to return to the original sin and "unlearn" the official history because, as Francisco Cantú writes, the "only true way to honor a place we love ... is to tell the fullness of its story". So let's tell that story – and perhaps consign everything we once thought we knew to history.

1

Contents

Unless stated otherwise, the photographs in this issue were taken by **Josh Edelson**, whose work illustrates the articles by Anna Wiener, Vanessa Hua, Michele Masneri, Mark Arax and, along with photographs by Nic Coury, Brian Goldstone. Josh is a photojournalist and advertising photographer living in the Bay Area. He has worked for leading publications and news agencies including Agence France-Presse, the Associated Press, Getty Images, the *Los Angeles Times* and *The Wall Street Journal*. Natural disasters are the leitmotif running through his work, particularly wildfires such as the Paradise fire – over the course of his career he has covered around a hundred – but also tornadoes, earthquakes, volcanic eruptions and floods. It is no coincidence that he has won a Covering Climate Now award. He was also a finalist in the News Photo Awards for his work on the Covid-19 pandemic in San Francisco.

Some Numbers

PROMISED LAND

— Population of California, millions
Percentage change from previous decade

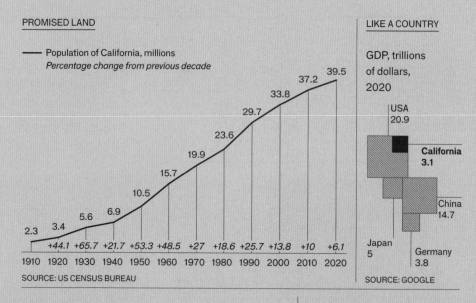

1910	1920	1930	1940	1950	1960	1970	1980	1990	2000	2010	2020
2.3	3.4	5.6	6.9	10.5	15.7	19.9	23.6	29.7	33.8	37.2	39.5
+44.1	+65.7	+21.7	+53.3	+48.5	+27	+18.6	+25.7	+13.8	+10	+6.1	

SOURCE: US CENSUS BUREAU

LIKE A COUNTRY

GDP, trillions of dollars, 2020

USA
20.9

**California
3.1**

China
14.7

Japan
5

Germany
3.8

SOURCE: GOOGLE

IMMIGRATION? YES, PLEASE

Does immigration in California have a positive or negative impact?

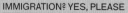

(%) ■ Negative   □ Positive   ▨ No response

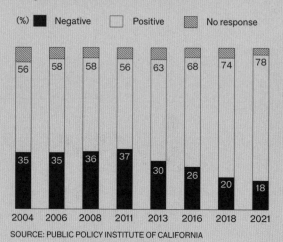

2004	2006	2008	2011	2013	2016	2018	2021
56	58	58	56	63	68	74	78
35	35	36	37	30	26	20	18

SOURCE: PUBLIC POLICY INSTITUTE OF CALIFORNIA

GDP PER CAPITA

GDP per capita in dollars, 2021

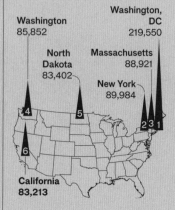

Washington
85,852

Washington, DC
219,550

North Dakota
83,402

Massachusetts
88,921

New York
89,984

California
83,213

SOURCE: WIKIPEDIA

MEGACOMPANIES

Top 10 stock-market-listed Californian companies by turnover (billions of dollars), 2020

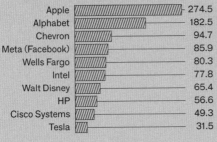

Apple	274.5
Alphabet	182.5
Chevron	94.7
Meta (Facebook)	85.9
Wells Fargo	80.3
Intel	77.8
Walt Disney	65.4
HP	56.6
Cisco Systems	49.3
Tesla	31.5

SOURCE: STATISTA

MAIN AGRICULTURAL PRODUCTS

California produces a third of all vegetables in the USA and two-thirds of the fresh fruit and dried fruit and nuts

The top 8 crops by value (millions of dollars), 2020

7.5 Milk and dairy	5.6 Almonds	4.5 Grapes	2.9 Pistachios
2.7 Cattle	2.3 Lettuce	1.9 Strawberries	1.2 Tomatoes

SOURCE: CALIFORNIA DEPARTMENT OF FOOD AND AGRICULTURE

ON THE WATERFRONT

Busiest ports in the western hemisphere by TEU (20-foot equivalent units, the standard container size), 2019

1

Los Angeles (California)
9,337

2

Long Beach (California)
7,632

3

New York (New York/New Jersey)
7,471

4

Colón (Panama)
4,379

5

Savannah (Georgia)
4,350

SOURCE: WIKIPEDIA

FOREST COVER

32.7%

A third of the state is forest, most of which is publicly managed

SOURCE: US DEPARTMENT OF AGRICULTURE

MENS SANA IN CORPORE SANO

Gym membership, percentage by state, 2019

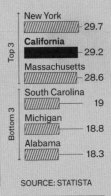

Top 3	New York	29.7
	California	29.2
	Massachusetts	28.6
Bottom 3	South Carolina	19
	Michigan	18.8
	Alabama	18.3

SOURCE: STATISTA

SEA-LEVEL RISE

Projected sea-level rise in San Diego (cm)

— Probable scenario (66% likely)
— Scenario with a 1-in-200 chance

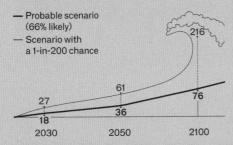

216
61
27
76
18
36
2030   2050   2100

SOURCE: LEGISLATIVE ANALYST'S OFFICE

AN UNENVIABLE RECORD

Number of mass shootings (4 or more victims) by state, 1982–2021

Washington 7
Wisconsin
Ohio 5
New York 4
Colorado 7
Pennsylvania 5
4 4
California 22
Illinois
Texas
11
Florida 12

SOURCE: STATISTA

DECALIFOR

FRANCESCO COSTA

Translated by Deborah Wassertzug
Photographs by David Paul Morris

A young man on an electric skateboard heads towards
the Bay Bridge, which links San Francisco with Oakland.

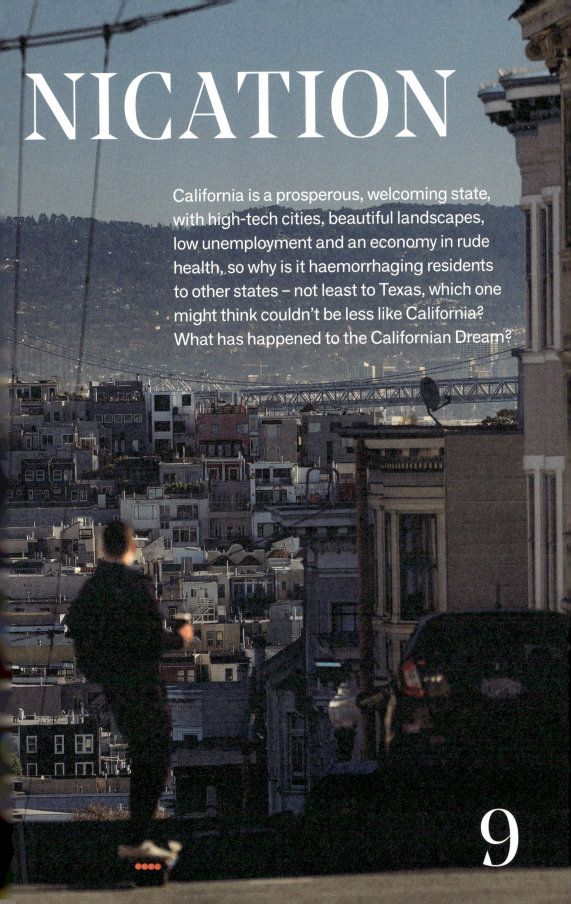

NICATION

California is a prosperous, welcoming state, with high-tech cities, beautiful landscapes, low unemployment and an economy in rude health, so why is it haemorrhaging residents to other states – not least to Texas, which one might think couldn't be less like California? What has happened to the Californian Dream?

In 2013 the then Republican governor of Texas, Rick Perry, bought thirty-second ad spots on California radio stations to deliver a very simple message: "Come check out Texas". The ads were principally aimed at seducing California's small-business owners, inviting them to look into the possibility of moving both themselves and their companies to his state. The initiative was noticed. All governors want to make their states seem attractive, but few of them run ad campaigns aimed at competing with one specific state. This move was met with sneers, however. The only selling point the adverts could highlight was Texas's noted leniency on tax laws for businesses. California at that point already had the fifth largest economy in the entire world – not exactly a place that was inhospitable to business. And, what is more, critics said, who would ever seriously consider leaving California – progressive, liberal, welcoming and fascinating – packing up their belongings and moving to Texas, that backward province of ultra-conservatives in wide-brimmed hats? Would they have to buy themselves a horse? When Jerry Brown, governor of California at that time, was asked what impact that ad campaign might have, his response was dismissive: "Barely a fart". Less than ten years have passed since then, but today there are few in California who would dare to be that arrogant.

The latest decennial census of the United States showed only a tiny increase in California's population, the smallest in its history; 2020 was the first time that California's population actually showed a decrease. The consequence was something that had never happened before: California lost a seat in the House of Representatives. Meanwhile, Texas gained two seats. Not bad for a fart. For years California has topped rankings of American states losing the most residents. Of course, it is hardly the worst-off state in the country, but these are rankings in which California had never before appeared. And yet, for some time now, over half a million people leave the state each year, many more than those arriving from the rest of the country and elsewhere in the world. Of these, over 600,000 people have, in fact, moved to Texas and with them the headquarters of huge and influential companies such as Hewlett-Packard, Tesla, Toyota and Oracle, along with hundreds of thousands of small and mid-sized companies. A nonprofit called the California Policy Center has decided to track this via an online spreadsheet that is constantly updated, entitled "The California Book of Exoduses". But the migration flow out of California goes far beyond Texas. Approximately one million people moved to Arizona from California between 2010 and 2018. Over fifty thousand people annually move to Nevada, whose population today consists of more adults born in California than in Nevada. Even Idaho is being invaded and transformed by Californians. Idaho, a state so utterly lacking in allure that the

FRANCESCO COSTA is an Italian journalist, blogger and essayist and deputy editor of the online newspaper *il Post*. Since 2015 he has been the author and presenter of *Da Costa a Costa*, a newsletter and podcast on US politics, society and culture. In 2019 he hosted the podcasts *Milano, Europa* and *The Big Seven*, in which he discusses seven notable contemporary Americans. He has published two books on the USA, *Questa è l'America* ("This Is America", Mondadori, 2020) and *Una storia americana* ("An American Story", Mondadori, 2021). Since 2021 he has presented the daily podcast *Morning* for *il Post*.

DAVID PAUL MORRIS is a photojournalist who has worked in Asia and America for more than twenty years. A well-travelled and established professional photographer, he collaborates with publications that view photography as an important tool for communication. His work covers stories and social issues from a number of angles for publications such as *Discover* magazine, *National Geographic*, *Newsweek*, *People*, *Stern*, *Time*, the *Los Angeles Times* and the *San Francisco Chronicle* and agencies Bloomberg News and Getty Images.

legend on its car licence plates – where other US states proudly declare the likes of "The Last Frontier" (Alaska), "The Sunshine State" (Florida), "Legendary" (North Dakota) and "Live Free or Die" (New Hampshire) – reads "Famous Potatoes". Idaho has potatoes. And, for a while now, a lot of Californians.

In theory, none of this should be happening. Except during wars and conflicts, in the modern world migrations almost always head in the direction of strong economies and employment; people leave places that offer fewer opportunities and go to places that offer more. How does California come into this? Leading economic indicators find its economy in perfect health: median income is high compared with the United States as a whole, and the unemployment rate is lower than the national average; work and opportunities are not in short supply.

California's economic prosperity is primarily based on the success of three enormous sectors around which many satellite businesses orbit: the technology industry, with its centre of gravity in the Bay Area, attracts investment from around the world and has changed the lives of every human being; the entertainment industry, both film and television, with extraordinarily far-reaching global influence, is centred on Los Angeles; and agriculture, which produces fruits and vegetables that reach every corner of the country. Then there are banking and finance (someone has to manage all this

wealth), tourism, the increasingly important wine industry, the oil industry and the solar-energy industry. More than any cold, hard socioeconomic data, however, it is California's historically symbolic and cultural position that highlights the anomaly of this situation. California has for centuries been considered to be the new frontier, home of the American Dream, ultimate goal of explorers of the West. It was, to all intents and purposes, the place one went to search for gold or escape poverty, even in the face of exhausting and dangerous migrations, such as the one John Steinbeck wrote about in *The Grapes of Wrath*. It was not only money that made California a magnet: its climate is inviting; its population comes from every corner of the globe; its culture is rich, lively, avant-garde and irreverent; and its geography is incredible. Hundreds of kilometres of beaches and cliffs facing the ocean, behind which are hills that seem to be a factory of computer-desktop images, surrounded by lakes and mountains, vast deserts and redwood forests. The promised land, literally. None of this has vanished, in spite of the worst drought of the century and the wildfires that each year consume between 1 and 2 per cent of the land surface of the state. No one has relocated Yosemite, and the Golden Gate Bridge is still amazing. Certainly, behind the data and far from the coasts, there is hardship: agriculture is beginning to feel the effects of the drought, while the largest inland cities, Fresno

> "The population of California has nearly doubled since 1980, its current stagnation notwithstanding. However, the building of new homes and apartment units has not grown at the same pace."

and Bakersfield, are American capitals of methamphetamine abuse. But there is nothing that would seem to justify the existence of companies that specialise in moving their customers from California to other nearby states and which have waiting lists for their services many months long. Or the dozens and dozens of Facebook groups with names like "Life After California" or "Move to Texas from California" that have tens of thousands of members. These groups provide information, advice and support to those wishing to make the big leap.

What happened to "California Dreamin'" and all that? The short answer is that California is going through a process of widespread gentrification, which Wikipedia defines as "the process of changing the character of a neighbourhood through the influx of more affluent residents and businesses". Typically, the phenomenon affects working-class areas, which undergo sudden changes and lose their identity through increases in the cost of living. This attracts newer, wealthier residents and prices out the middle class, and it is happening within a state that is much larger than Germany, inhabited by around forty million people. Things are more complicated than this, as we will see in a moment, but it is worth beginning at the starting point of every gentrification story: the home.

*

The population of California has nearly doubled since 1980, its current stagnation notwithstanding. However, the building of new homes and apartment units has not grown at the same pace. Neither money nor space are lacking for their construction but rather the political will to do so. Over the years cities have approved increasingly restrictive zoning regulations, with the stated goal being to protect the historic identity of their communities (see "A Home of One's Own" on page 15). In reality, the goal is to safeguard the interests of existing homeowners who do not relish the idea of construction sites right outside their front doors and who fear, even more, that the building of new homes in their neighbourhoods might lower the value of the existing properties and bring in new neighbours from different ethnic groups and social classes. With few exceptions, the only building projects in California that manage to respect both town-planning regulations and overcome the much feared and often constraining residents' consultations are those for new single-family or two-family homes: those classic detached houses with gardens that fit in with the American suburban landscape, which cost a lot and represent particularly inefficient land use, especially in a state that is experiencing a dramatic housing crisis.

Politicians are trying to put a sticking plaster on it after decades of inaction: in September 2021 a state law was passed permitting the construction of two-family houses (also called duplexes) on land originally zoned for single-family homes and permitting the transformation of

Homes for sale
and under construction
in Oakland and San
Francisco.

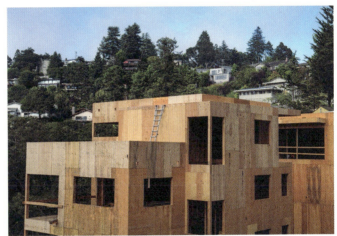

A demonstration in Sunnyvale outside the building where the annual general meeting of Google's parent company, Alphabet, was taking place. Workers and activists were protesting over a series of issues, including contractors' rights and the tech giant's activities in China.

At the root of many of California's problems – from the housing crisis to growing urban sprawl in fire-risk areas – lies the American Dream of the detached family home, a dream fiercely defended by those who have made it a reality by means of development plans that are often discriminatory. "Single-family zoning", which sets aside an area exclusively for detached family homes (and therefore rules out terraces, duplexes or apartments), is a Californian invention – with clear segregationist origins. It is thought to have emerged first in Elmwood, Berkeley, where in 1916 a real-estate developer had a single-family zoning plan approved in order to keep out Black and Chinese residents – who were not in a position to afford that type of housing – and thus ensure the value of the properties he was trying to sell were maintained. The Supreme Court subsequently declared explicitly segregationist development plans unconstitutional but had nothing to say about single-family zoning, which became the norm in the United States and particularly in California, where almost three-quarters of building land is subdivided into single-family zones (a figure that rises to 94 per cent in San Jose). Since 2021 there have been attempts to change direction, first on a municipal level – fittingly enough in Berkeley where it all began – and then on a state level, with Senate Bill 9, which effectively eliminates single-family zoning. The law's impact will probably be limited, however, because it will suit only a small proportion of owners to convert their homes into duplexes. An estimated 700,000 new units will be created, which is a fifth of the total of around 3.5 million homes believed to be needed.

single-family homes into duplexes, an option that promises to be very tempting for those intending to sell. Something is changing, in other words, but it will take some time before the limited effects of this change are felt. This is also because the housing crisis in California is aggravated by real-estate taxes; these came about following a controversial referendum in 1978 (see "Proposition 13" on page 21), which established that property owners could not be taxed more than 1 per cent of the market value of their buildings and, furthermore, that the market value would only be updated at the moment of an eventual sale. Given that every sale involved an appreciation in the value of a property, after this referendum was approved, selling a home and buying another became much less advantageous. The market has atrophied, and home prices are out of reach of the middle class. There are fewer homes than required, and fewer are being built than are needed. Home sales are rare and punishingly expensive. The result: an overall increase in prices both for renters and buyers. Since 2008 house prices per square metre in Los Angeles, San Diego and San Francisco have risen by 70, 80 and 116 per cent respectively. Renting a room in San Francisco averages $2,700 per month – with the key words here being "room" and "average". The market for sublets is ferocious and poorly regulated: people quite literally lose their housing overnight. The competition Airbnb has brought to the hotels sector has made things even worse by removing more rooms from the rental market.

The stories those who live in California – and those who have left it – tell about the state's housing market are nothing if not surreal. There's the Berkeley student who manages to pay for tuition at one of the

In 1967 the University of California, Berkeley, bought a plot of land, planning to demolish the existing houses and to erect student accommodation. Demolition began in 1968, but the university ran out of funds, leaving a muddy wasteland. When work had not restarted by the following year hundreds of students occupied the land, planting trees and flowers, laying turf and naming it the People's Park. But the new park was short-lived: on 15 May 1969 the then governor of California, Ronald Reagan, sent in heavily armed National Guard troopers to evict them, equipped with trucks and helicopters. In what became known as "Bloody Thursday", more than a hundred occupiers were injured, some very seriously, and one was killed. Over the following decades, despite numerous attempts, the park has still not been redeveloped and is now home to a few people who have holed up there since 2020 when the encampment bans were suspended during the pandemic: numbers of homeless people in California are soaring, along with petty crime, and Berkeley is no exception. Rents are extremely high, and only 40 per cent of students live in the city (the lowest percentage for any US university). To tackle the problem the university has promised to build new rent-controlled student accommodation in People's Park and set up a memorial to commemorate the events of 1969. But there is opposition to the plans, with claims that the initiative will not go far enough to solve the issues affecting the park or students.

most prestigious and expensive universities in the world but sleeps in People's Park adjacent to the campus. There's the nurse who is forced to commute two hours each way by car every day because the only solution to insane prices – and the near absence of good public transport – is to move far away from cities. There's the police officer who prefers to sleep in his car when his shifts are scheduled close together, because if he had to go home in the evening only to return to the station in the morning he would get only two hours' sleep. The mass-commuter lifestyle produces unimaginable traffic and worsens air quality: the six most polluted cities in the USA are in California. Cities have introduced preferential carpool (or HOV, high-occupancy-vehicle) lanes on highways for cars with more than one passenger – another well-intentioned idea that has made things worse. Moving across such a vast area so slowly, taking two or three times as long to reach two or three different destinations means spending even more time in traffic, leaving the house earlier to adjust for it and risking arriving at work late because of an accident or sudden traffic jam. So, few cars use the preferential lanes while the other lanes are beyond jammed. The desperation is such that every so often someone is pulled over on a carpool lane with a mannequin in the passenger seat in a desperate attempt to trick the highway police and save a half hour.

It doesn't take much to get evicted from your home in a housing system like this one, especially since, compared with standards in Europe, labour laws in the United States are weak and it is easy to let employees go. Those evicted from their homes end up on the street, and for years now even tourists have noticed it: the number of homeless people in California's urban areas is shocking, with entire neighbourhoods turned into tent cities.

Given all that, the choice to leave the state might no longer sound quite such a foolish one. A single-family home in San Diego costs $725,000, while in Fort Worth, Texas, it costs $260,000 and is perhaps just a ten-minute drive from work instead of three hours. People can rent a house with a garden in Arizona for the same amount they spend on a two-room apartment in Los Angeles. A person selling a home in California can buy three houses in Idaho. Today San Francisco is inhabited mainly by the ultra-rich, who are more numerous there than anywhere else in the country. The percentage of African-American inhabitants, however, has dropped from 13 per cent to 5 per cent in fifty years. San Francisco is perhaps the only place in America which has become more white, not less, with the passage of time. And it is mostly middle-class families who are leaving. The median age of California residents today is forty and is rising much more quickly than in the rest of the country. In San Francisco there are fewer residents under the age of eighteen than in any other large city in the USA. In Los Angeles that same population has dropped by 17 per cent in the past ten years. Even birth rates are declining, for obvious reasons, while the population becomes progressively more white, older and less numerous. And richer.

*

The story might end here: this is why so many people have left California. But in such a vast and complex society every mass phenomenon has infinite ramifications, some impossible to investigate and some more obvious. Everything costs more in California, from the water and electricity bills to rubbish collection or a simple meal in a restaurant. Crime rates are already high and rising, Californian public schools do not score highly in national rankings, and during the summer there are regular power outages. The company in charge of the electrical grid is Pacific Gas and Electric, made infamous by the story of Erin Brockovich. It is one of the most corrupt and inefficient utilities in the country. Rolling blackouts are meant to keep strong winds from knocking down towers in forests and starting new wildfires that would make the air even less breathable. In spite of these precautions – if we can call them that – the company filed for bankruptcy in 2019 because of the huge numbers of compensation payments due to victims of fires caused by the company's negligence. Remember the photos from 2020 of the orange skies over San Francisco? The following year the smoke and ash even reached New York, two time zones away.

But let's return to the referendum of 1978, the one that reduced taxes on property – and which perhaps provides a partial explanation as to why certain countries, including my own, Italy, prefer to exclude budget issues from those questions that can be directly voted on by the population. A significant portion of California's annual budget is not controlled by politicians: money is spent the way the population has decided it should be spent through referendums approved years ago – and in the spirit of those times – in conditions very different from today's. And it is simply too bad if those choices no longer make sense today, assuming they did even back then. In 1988, for example, teachers' unions proposed in Proposition 98 to allocate at least 40 per cent of the state's total budget to education – every year, regardless of the needs of the school system or of the economic

A view over the Sunset District of San Francisco. In 2020 property taxes in the USA increased at the fastest pace for four years, with some of the steepest increases coming in traditionally low cost Sun Belt states.

THE PASSENGER   Francesco Costa

situation – without stating where and how those funds might be sourced. But who would ever oppose funding education in progressive, liberal California? The referendum was approved, and so over the years in this same way were many others. The need to find and free up resources in the face of the sequestering of all these funds has led to steep increases in taxes. In California there are taxes that do not even exist in other states, and income tax is extremely high compared with the rest of the country, not only for the very rich, who find ways to get around paying them anyway, but most of all for the middle class. Someone who earns $58,000 a year in California is taxed on that income at double the rate that someone in Arizona earning the same amount would be. A family with an annual total household income of between $100,000 and $200,000 is taxed at a higher rate in California than in any other American state. Although this fact is now widely known, until a number of years ago families who moved to Texas were astounded when they discovered that income tax simply did not exist in their new home. Zero. The same went for business owners when they found out that the minimum wage – $14 per hour in California; $16 per hour in San Francisco – in Texas is still tied to the national rate of $7.25 an hour. Of course, paying lower taxes means having fewer services, and the level of public services in Texas cannot be compared with that of California. But the economic growth of recent years has mitigated the consequences of this disparity, and many of those who leave are so frustrated by the intrusiveness and inefficiency of local government in California that they even find the minimal and laissez-faire ways of Texas seductive.

While these two states might seem as different as two states can be – and, indeed, in many ways they are – the cultural and historical similarities between them should not be overlooked. California and Texas are the two largest US states, and those with the strongest and most solid identities. They both like to think they are nations unto themselves instead of being part of a larger union. They almost always vote in opposite directions, but historical evolution shows how the granite binary logic of any winner-takes-all political system hides just how much more complex and multifaceted societies and cultures actually are. Until the 1970s Texas almost exclusively had Democratic governors. It is the state that President Lyndon B. Johnson came from, the man who abolished racial segregation and introduced the most ambitious welfare programmes that the United States has ever known, Medicaid and Medicare.

In California, by contrast, Republicans had a glorious past in government and with national influence. Does the name Ronald Reagan ring any bells? Both California and Texas also have significant Latin American presences – both states, at various points in their histories, were governed by Spain and Mexico – and both have a conflicted relationship with anything that might be considered "power" or central authority. In Texas this takes the form of libertarian impatience with Washington, its terror of the "nanny state" and its desire for a government that does the least amount possible. Meanwhile in California it takes different forms: the frequent recourse to direct democracy, which can even recall elected officers before the end of their term, as was the risk in September 2021 to current governor Gavin Newsom; in the influence of many citizens' committees (California boasts organisations for almost any cause, often more than one for each); in the formidable liveliness, influence and richness of what used to be called the counterculture; in the desire of every startup to "disrupt" a market, not just the established competitors but the rules that regulate the market itself. (Uber is a good example.) The sense of cultural oppression that a significant number of people in California experience is accentuated by the now decades-long dominance of the Democratic Party, which eliminates the accountability of local politicians. If a Democratic politician does a poor job, the most that can happen is that they are replaced by another Democratic politician. This systematically keeps conservative voters out of play, preventing them from having true representation and therefore no impact whatsoever on local politics. In a majority system a victory is declared with an absolute majority, and the minority gets zero even if it comprises 30 or 40 per cent of the population. Furthermore, on a cultural level, if there were a place in the world where it would make the most sense to speak of "excesses of political correctness" and "cancel culture" without recalling the fear mongering scattergunned in every direction by the extreme right, that place would be California. The extreme speed with which the bar is raised in matters of behaviour and speech considered sensitive, inclusive and tolerant – and, above all, behaviour and speech which from one day

PROPOSITION 13

California has not always been a liberal stronghold, and its conservative past has left a disproportionate legacy, at least in terms of taxation – notably, the state gave rise to the first populist anti-tax uprising, which many believe was a crucial factor in the election of Ronald Reagan to the presidency in 1980. In California the revolt culminated in 1978 with Proposition 13, the initiative put forward by Howard Jarvis, a 75-year-old who has been described as a precursor to Donald Trump and features in Jason Cohn and Camille Servan-Schreiber's 2019 documentary *The First Angry Man*. (This being California, Jarvis also made a cameo appearance in the 1980 comedy *Airplane!*) Riding a wave of discontent among homeowners at a time of rising inflation, particularly for white pensioners on a fixed income who were no longer able to afford their bills, Jarvis gained 63 per cent support to pass his measure capping property taxes (residential and commercial) at 1 per cent and limiting annual increases to the rate of inflation, subject to a maximum of 2 per cent. According to its critics, Proposition 13 favours long-standing owners – properties are only revalued when they are sold – and the elderly at the expense of the young, but the major beneficiaries are companies and the owners of commercial properties. In spite of its detrimental effects on the real-estate market, the amendment to the constitution remains popular, and no politician dares call it into question, helped by the fact that it can only be changed with a two-thirds majority in both houses.

Residential developments in Hercules. Two laws signed by Gavin Newsom, the governor of California, have opened the doors to "upzoning" in traditionally single-family neighbourhoods, allowing the creation of more residential units.

to the next is no longer considered to be so – is matched in the professional and social spheres by increasingly severe sanctions imposed on anyone found not to be up to speed on the latest circular. Some months ago, for example, a professor of Chinese at the University of Southern California was reprimanded and replaced because, during a class, he had said "*ne ga*", a filler in Chinese that sounded like the unsayable N-word. Elsewhere, school districts are even discussing rebranding schools named after Abraham Lincoln, the most venerated president in US history, who ended the Civil War and abolished slavery. The idea of packing up and moving to Texas for many people seems like opening a window and taking a big gulp of fresh air – a feeling reinforced by the lack of any Californian cities on the list of top fifty US cities with the most green space per capita. And if Texas seems too extreme, there's always Arizona, Nevada or Colorado.

*

California's problems would never be enough on their own to drag such a significant portion of the population out of a state so well off it even has a populous county that is literally called El Dorado. There must have been something outside of California exerting an attractive force that presents Californians with an alternative that, despite big upheavals, wouldn't mean real sacrifice or hardship. The economic history of the United States in the past twenty years, especially since the Great Recession of 2008, is the story of a recovery that took place principally in southern and western states.

The Texan economy, at one time based almost exclusively on oil and livestock, is much more diversified and modern today. The influence of oil has gradually slipped, and yet its GDP has continued to grow, driven by the pharmaceutical, IT, aerospace and defence sectors. Then there are sources of growth and prosperity that were previously unthinkable in those parts, such as culture and tourism. The city of Austin symbolises this transformation: it hosts the Texas Book Festival, one of the largest in the country, and South by Southwest (SXSW), which has been for some time the premier event in the arts (music and film), technology and innovation sectors. But similar things could be said about San Antonio and Houston, or about Phoenix, Arizona, or Denver, Colorado, and many other mid-sized cities: demographic and economic expansion on a large scale, ethnic diversification, lively culture and unfettered housing development.

This brings us to a dilemma that recalls the chicken and the egg, one to which Americans never manage a response: how many of the changes in the states in the south and west of the United States – the changes making them gradually more modern, more welcoming and richer, especially the cities – how many of these changes can be attributed to the arrival of all these Californians? On the other hand, how much of this development is what is attracting Californians and convincing them to take the big leap? Who is changing whom? It will likely be some time before we can answer this question, assuming there is only one answer. Perhaps both are true. Political and voting data, for example, demonstrate unequivocally that while Californians are moving en masse to the states in the Southwest, those same states are slowly becoming less conservative and more progressive. The mid-sized and large cities in the region today are all governed by Democrats. This is even the case in Texas, where in 2018 noted extreme-right

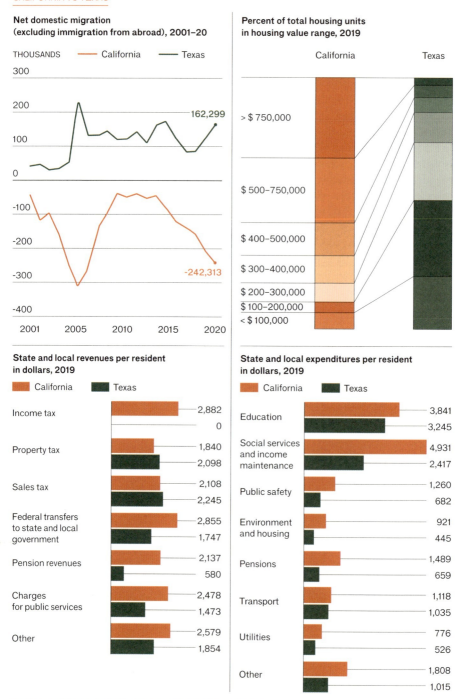

**Net domestic migration
(excluding immigration from abroad), 2001–20**

THOUSANDS — California — Texas

162,299

-242,313

2001   2005   2010   2015   2020

**Percent of total housing units
in housing value range, 2019**

California   Texas

> $ 750,000

$ 500–750,000

$ 400–500,000

$ 300–400,000

$ 200–300,000
$ 100–200,000
< $ 100,000

**State and local revenues per resident
in dollars, 2019**

■ California   ■ Texas

	California	Texas
Income tax	2,882	0
Property tax	1,840	2,098
Sales tax	2,108	2,245
Federal transfers to state and local government	2,855	1,747
Pension revenues	2,137	580
Charges for public services	2,478	1,473
Other	2,579	1,854

**State and local expenditures per resident
in dollars, 2019**

■ California   ■ Texas

	California	Texas
Education	3,841	3,245
Social services and income maintenance	4,931	2,417
Public safety	1,260	682
Environment and housing	921	445
Pensions	1,489	659
Transport	1,118	1,035
Utilities	776	526
Other	1,808	1,015

SOURCE: STANFORD INSTITUTE FOR ECONOMIC POLICY RESEARCH

> "The idea of packing up and moving to Texas for many people seems like opening a window and taking a big gulp of fresh air."

senator Ted Cruz was re-elected by barely 2 percentage points and where contested elections between Republican and Democratic candidates are no longer a rarity. Arizona, once the domain of the Republican Party, chose Joe Biden in 2020 and today boasts two Democratic senators. Nevada, in the south of which California-born voters outnumber native Nevadan voters three to one, has voted for Democratic candidates for president since 2008. The same has occurred in Colorado, where Republicans once won hands down. Democrats are recouping in the south and west what they are losing in Midwestern states of heavy industry, large labour unions and working-class whites, once their stronghold. American political geography has changed.

Is everyone happy then? More or less. The states to which Californians have fled have experienced strong economic growth in recent years, pulled by housing development – those areas are in the midst of a construction boom – and by demographic growth. Californians, in fact, arrive and Californianise: they vote for progressive politicians, they organise cultural initiatives and they make themselves heard in school districts and local organisations. Creating new demand and bringing with them the supply, they change the places to which they go: small semi-abandoned city centres lost in the countryside suddenly have bars with live music and hipster cafés on street corners. The pandemic has accelerated these transformations, freeing many people from the need to head to an office every day. But it is growth that is beginning to cause the same problems that Californians sought to escape: increased housing and living costs, gentrification, the forcing out of poorer residents and an increase in economic inequality. Conservative politicians are the ones who find themselves in the most ambiguous and complex positions: on the one hand, they try to take credit for this economic development; on the other, they want to avoid having the Californians pull the rug out from under them (the current governor of Texas, Greg Abbott, used as a campaign slogan "Don't California My Texas"). But even local populations feel a growing sense of unease. In Idaho there are cities where housing costs have doubled in five years, and there is graffiti on walls reading "Californians go home" and "Go back to Cali". The alarming fact, if we broaden our view, is that the problems of California are ones found in many other places in the United States, even if at the moment they are less acute. These are, paradoxically, places where things seem to be going better from an economic standpoint. When examining this strange crisis of California – one that worsens in spite of losing increasing numbers of residents and which has failed to reduce inequality despite the state's economic success – the lingering conclusion is that, beyond local specifics, the phenomenon has deeper roots. It is clear that ambitious interventions are required in order to keep California's present from becoming a particularly brutal version of the future that awaits capitalism throughout the United States. 🐦

Three Kids, Two Paychecks, No Home

In Salinas, Monterey County, a fertile corner of California that produces much of the food consumed in the USA, soaring housing costs mean working families end up sleeping in shelters and parking lots. The journalist and anthropologist Brian Goldstone meets Brenda and Candido and their kids, a family forced to live in their minivan and suffer the cascading effects of homelessness.

BRIAN GOLDSTONE
Photographs by Josh Edelson and Nic Coury

A homeless encampment opposite San Francisco's City Hall. With the surge in homelessness, city officials put aside an area for around fifty tents, properly distanced, with 24-hour monitoring and portable bathroom facilities, to help reduce the spread of Covid-19.

Frankie's morning started before the sun came up, as the steadily increasing volume of his parents' phone alarm, coming from somewhere near the dashboard, jolted the eight-year-old awake. His dad Candido and six-year-old brother Josephat had begun to stir in the cramped rear of the minivan, emerging from a tangle of blankets, towels, pillows, and stuffed animals. His mom Brenda was in the driver's seat, which was reclined as far back as it could go; his baby sister Adelene, who was three, was splayed out awkwardly on the seat beside her. As for Frankie, he was in his usual spot: nestled on the floorboard between the front seats and middle row, his skinny four-foot (1.2-meter) frame hidden in a furry green-and-brown sleeping bag meant to look like a grizzly bear.

For almost nine months the family had been living out of their Toyota Sienna in various fields and parking lots throughout Salinas, the industrial and economic center of Monterey County. In this part of the country, there was nothing especially dramatic or exceptional about their plight or the circumstances that led them to be without a roof over their heads. Frankie's parents were well aware of the worsening housing crisis that had dragged tens of thousands of Californians into a similar fate. But still, Candido said, it sometimes felt as though they were the only ones out there.

Finding a place to park the van was harder than expected. At first, the family tried the parking lot of a Food 4 Less grocery store. But, the following morning, an employee warned them not to return; a neighborhood gang, he explained, controlled the area and had been threatening homeless people. He said they'd recently slashed someone's tires. The family drove to a nearby strawberry farm, which proved more hospitable. In exchange for doing chores around the property, such as cleaning the bathrooms and emptying the trash, the farm's owner would fill up their gas tank. But eventually other families, in their own cars and SUVs, began showing up, and it became too much. They'd have to go somewhere else, the owner said.

Now they were in the parking lot of Natividad Medical Center, just outside the emergency room. The lot was well lit, and there were bathrooms in the ER waiting room, open twenty-four hours. The hospital staff was mostly welcoming. At night, however, after everyone fell asleep, Candido had been noticing the tiny flicker of a lighter in a nearby pickup truck and the profile of an older man. Candido kept the van's dome light on and made sure its doors were locked.

As parents, Candido and Brenda believed the most important thing was to project confidence; their kids needed to see that they had a plan. The couple tried to avoid worrying about how long they'd be in the van or where they might go next, but it was impossible to think

BRIAN GOLDSTONE is an American journalist and cultural anthropologist whose reports and essays have appeared in *Harper's*, *The New Republic*, *The California Sunday Magazine*, *Guernica*, *Jacobin* and *Public Books*. He is director of In the Press, a journalism and public humanities writing initiative at Duke University's Franklin Humanities Institute, and in 2015–16, as a Justice-in-Education Fellow at Columbia University, he taught in Sing Sing prison. His forthcoming book, *The New American Homeless*, investigates the crisis of housing insecurity in US cities and the dramatic rise of the working homeless.

NIC COURY is a Monterey-based photojournalist and portrait photographer. They are non-binary, and part of their work focuses on stories from the LGBTQ+ community. They are a contributor to the Associated Press, *The New York Times*, the *San Francisco Chronicle*, the *Los Angeles Times*, *The Washington Post* among others and have made commercial photos for Red Bull, Ferrari and Bugatti. In their spare time they are an obsessed chicken owner, gardener, surfer and climber.

about anything else. There were bouts of cursing and storming off and feeling that one more minute in the vehicle, packed with the entirety of their possessions, would drive them all insane. There were weekend excursions to the budget store Target for little toys and treats, bought with money they couldn't spare. When temperatures dropped, it was a terrible calculus: bundle up as best they could, the kids shivering and complaining, or run the van's heater all night and use up precious gas. Or, if there were any rooms available, they could spend up to a couple hundred dollars a night at the Best 5 Motel or Good Nite Inn, making it that much less likely that they'd save enough to get out of the van entirely.

Mornings were the hardest. Everyone was achy, tired from a bad night's sleep, and on this morning, too, it was all they could do to keep to their routine. Brenda and Candido insisted on maintaining a semblance of order. "We're not like some people," Candido would tell the kids. "We wash our clothes. We don't pee outside. We keep ourselves clean." In the hospital bathroom, while Candido got ready to go to work and Brenda stayed behind with Adelene, Frankie helped wash and dress Josephat, brushing his brother's teeth then his own. Breakfast was whatever Pop-Tarts or granola bars were left over from the food bank. Finally, they straightened up the van, pulled the seats back into position, and put on their seat belts, Adelene in her car seat, Frankie and Josephat in their boosters. They drove the fifteen or

so minutes into town, fusing with the early traffic, indistinguishable from all the other families starting their day.

When the van stopped, the boys hopped out. They went around to the trunk, grabbed their backpacks off the built-in clothing hooks, hugged their parents, and walked through the front gate of their elementary school.

*

Traveling the length of Route 68, a twenty-mile (thirty-kilometer) road running from Asilomar State Beach in Pacific Grove to South Main Street in downtown Salinas, is like going from one version of California to another. On the Monterey Peninsula side of the "lettuce curtain" (as the invisible barrier separating Salinas from richer neighboring towns is often called) are exclusive beach communities, famous golf courses such as Pebble Beach, and a thriving tourism industry; at the opposite end of the highway, a working-class city with a poverty rate well above the state average.

Not that the Salinas Valley is lacking in beauty or natural resources. Long ago declared the "salad bowl of the world," the area's vast farms produce roughly two-thirds of the country's lettuce and much of our celery, cauliflower, wine grapes, broccoli, and strawberries. Its $8 billion agricultural economy—driven by corporate giants such as Dole, Taylor Farms, Driscoll's, Tanimura & Antle, and Earthbound Farm—has made the valley a place of immense wealth. But it's also

> **"The perverse irony that 'The Valley That Feeds the Nation,' the title of a colorful mural in nearby Soledad, is now struggling to feed itself has been lost on nobody."**

a place where battles over the distribution of this wealth have been fought for generations. In 1936, John Steinbeck, who was born in Salinas, noted in his non-fiction work *The Harvest Gypsies* the "curious attitude toward a group that makes our agriculture successful. The migrants are needed, and they are hated." Nearly four decades later, in the summer of 1970, Cesar Chavez and his United Farm Workers helped organize a massive strike against the valley's growers, which effectively shut down the lettuce industry (see "Cesar Chavez" on page 33). Previously, no safety, health, or labor laws protected these workers, and they could be fired at will; now the farms—what Chavez proudly referred to as "liberated ranches"—were forced to provide better pay and working conditions for the men and women in their fields.

Today, the region's 91,000 farmworkers live with stagnant wages (the median pay for farmworkers is $12.79 per hour) and the constant threat of the US Immigration and Customs Enforcement agency (ICE; the majority of these laborers are undocumented). Public health officials describe an epidemic of malnutrition among the workers and their families, and hunger has become widespread. The perverse irony that "The Valley That Feeds the Nation," the title of a colorful mural in nearby Soledad, is now struggling to feed itself has been lost on nobody. Activists argue that a lack of fair wages in agriculture in particular is a key driver of this food insecurity. But for now, charity is what the industry is willing to offer. In 2018, at the Food Bank of Monterey County, much of the twelve million pounds (5.5 million kilograms) of emergency food assistance it provided was donated by agricultural companies.

By far the greatest difficulty facing Salinas families, though, is the disappearance of affordable rental housing. In recent years, tech workers from the Bay Area have been relocating to Monterey County, and there are currently plans for a commuter rail line that would run from the heart of Silicon Valley to Salinas. This influx of higher-earning tenants into an already congested market has led to a rise in rents, which, in turn—together with the exclusionary zoning, no-fault evictions, and barriers to new construction that have beleaguered the rest of the state—is creating unprecedented housing instability among Salinas's working poor. Over the past decade, there has been a 37 per cent loss of low-rent units in the city, while rents have shot up by almost 60 per cent since 2014—roughly four times the national average. According to the National Low Income Housing Coalition, the "housing wage" necessary to afford a modest two-bedroom apartment in Salinas, where costs now exceed those of Miami and Chicago, is $29.62 per hour.

The difficult daily lives of many homeless people in Salinas and San Francisco.

Increasingly, the city's residents have found themselves bereft of adequate shelter altogether. "There's always been poverty here," said Reyes Bonilla, who runs Community Homeless Solutions, a local nonprofit. "But homelessness on this scale? It's an entirely new thing." He added that many of those coming to his organization for support defy the stereotypes about homelessness; the vast majority of them are working and have simply been priced out of a place to live. Families are doubling and tripling up in overcrowded, substandard conditions; they're resorting to garages and toolsheds, cars and abandoned properties. In Monterey County, approximately eight thousand schoolchildren were homeless in 2018, more than San Francisco and San Jose combined. For many of these kids, the safest, most dependable part of their lives is the school they attend.

*

When Brenda and Candido first got together in 2014, they were still under the impression that if they worked hard enough they would be able to provide for their family. They met at a slaughterhouse in Dodge City, Kansas. Brenda, who was born in Belize, moved to Kansas with her family as an infant. Candido ended up there when his mom, fearful that her teenage son could be killed by rival gang members in Salinas after being shot at several times, sent him to stay with relatives in the Midwest. "I was in a really bad place back then," said Candido. By the time their paths crossed at the National Beef processing plant—he was a "chuck boner"; she was assigned to the packaging unit—Candido had become a committed Christian and was ready for a relationship. Brenda, for her part, had two young boys, was reeling from a painful break-up, had grown estranged from her parents,

and believed that the surest route to a better future lay in joining the Marines. Gradually Candido managed to convince her otherwise. "I saw how much he adored Frankie and Josephat," Brenda said. "I could tell he was very serious about being with us." Soon Candido was referring to the boys as his adopted sons, and, as it became clear that there was little left for them in Kansas, they agreed that going to California was their best option.

In the fall of 2016, the four of them moved into a small apartment in north Salinas, a safe neighborhood by the city's standards (at the time, Salinas had one of the highest murder rates in the US). Candido and Brenda, joking that they were destined to work together for the rest of their lives, landed jobs in the frozen-burrito factory at Sweet Earth Foods, a local vegan and vegetarian company, and were thrilled to be pulling in $15.25 per hour before taxes—more than they could have hoped to make in Dodge City. Yet rent and utilities alone were swallowing up over half their income. When Adelene was born and Brenda stopped working for a brief season to stay home with her, they realized that their financial footing was less secure than it had seemed. So they were grateful to accept an offer from Candido's mom to come stay with her. She had extra space, the location was more convenient, and, crucially, they would have help with childcare.

There was one catch. Owned and operated by the Housing Authority of the County of Monterey, the complex had strict rules governing who could reside in its units—and since the apartment was in Candido's mother's name, her children and grandchildren were barred from living there. The building's sympathetic manager, however, assured them that it would be fine; with a waiting list several

Born in Arizona in 1927, Cesar Chavez started work as a farm labourer as a child. In 1962 he became one of the founders of the National Farm Workers Association, a trade union composed predominantly of workers of Mexican origin. In 1965 the NFWA merged with another union to form the United Farm Workers during a major strike in Delano. Chavez joined after being encouraged by his representatives and immediately took charge, organising the strikers' march to Sacramento. As the head of the UFW he began an intense period of activity, inspired by Gandhi's methods of non-violent non-cooperation. He had great success with the grape boycott he started in the San Joaquin Valley, where a battle with the landowners was under way. It began in 1968 and lasted two years, gaining national coverage and achieving its desired aims. The marches, pickets and boycotts made Chavez's name, earning him an almost messianic reputation (Bobby Kennedy dubbed him "one of the heroic figures of our time"), although the result was a sort of cult of personality to which he responded with autocratic leadership of the union, purging dissidents whom he accused of spying. In spite of the controversies, his activism improved conditions for Californian labourers, particularly when Jerry Brown, who had marched with Chavez, became state governor and implemented union demands at a legislative level in 1974: minimum wages were raised and labourers won rights that would have been unthinkable not long before. However, these were years of decline for the UFW, which had lost members and its revolutionary spirit and whose leader was, by that point, behaving questionably.

years long even to enter the lottery for these subsidized rentals, they certainly weren't the only ones, he said, who'd be living "off-lease." Everything went well for about a year, but then a neighbor threatened to report the family. She'd started photographing the kids as they left and re-entered the apartment each day, and the manager had no choice but to tell them to go elsewhere. "We were totally scared and shocked," Brenda said, "and we knew that we needed to get out right away. If not, Candido's mom might have been evicted, too."

The timing couldn't have been worse. Temporarily relieved of the heavy burden of rent, Candido and Brenda, who was now working again, felt that their most pressing need was a car; since arriving in Salinas, they had been dependent on friends and relatives and city buses for transportation. By December 2018, they finally had enough money to purchase a 2007 minivan for $5,000—which also meant that, less than a month later, when they were forced to move, nearly all of their savings had been depleted. It would take a few months, maybe more, before they could afford the security deposit and first month's rent for an apartment.

Panicked, they went to the only place they could think of: a downtown homeless shelter. Originally intended as an emergency warming center during the winter months, the shelter—a seventy-person-capacity building that used to be a public defender's office—had become a year-round fixture for Salinas's growing homeless population. There were no showers, and everyone had to leave in the morning and line up again in the early evening, but there were hot meals, volunteer tutors to help with homework, and it offered protection from the Central Coast's frigid winter weather. An

> "The following days saw them exhaust every other option at their disposal. They tried camping at the beach. 'Think of it as an adventure,' they told the kids."

incident a few hours after they arrived, however, prevented them from staying at the shelter. Josephat, who has a developmental delay, was trying to get another boy his age to play with him; when that boy turned away, Josephat grabbed him by the hood of his sweatshirt and caused him to slip, smacking his head against the floor. The boy's parents were furious, and Candido and Brenda were asked to leave. The family slept outside in their new van.

Soon they were confronted with an alarming fact: there was one facility in the city where homeless families could find short-term relief, and they had just been kicked out of it. "It was awful," Candido said. "The van's tiny enclosed space was very hard for the kids. But it hit us that there was nowhere else to go." The following days saw them exhaust every other option at their disposal. They tried camping at the beach. "Think of it as an adventure," they told the kids. But, without a tent, they were freezing and miserable. They went into debt, borrowing what little money friends and family members could lend them—a hundred dollars here, two hundred there. Candido's sister, who lived in the same Housing Authority complex as their mom, wanted to offer her apartment to them, but they decided it was too risky. Even motel vacancies were hard to come by; local farms had started reserving whole blocks of rooms for their seasonal workers, driving up rates and, on many nights, filling up the motels.

As weeks turned into months, their situation became a case study in the cascading effects of homelessness. The stress of living in the van was compounded by their need to find a secure place to sleep and remain hidden from the authorities. Unlike some California cities where "safe parking lots" had been established for their unhoused and displaced residents, Salinas had nothing of the sort. In fact, it was illegal to sleep in a vehicle on public land.

Meanwhile, Josephat's behavior was worsening; he was more aggressive, more likely to lash out physically. This put everyone on edge, especially Brenda. From the time she was a teenager, she had been afflicted with severe panic attacks. Lately, the episodes were happening with greater frequency, and she was becoming withdrawn. Fearing that her anxiety was being triggered, in part, by the trouble Josephat was getting into, Candido requested that the school call him not Brenda if there were any problems. Before long he was receiving two or three calls a week, asking him to pick Josephat up right away: his son had thrown his food tray in the cafeteria, or refused to sit down in class, or punched a teacher. Candido's manager at work grew exasperated by these abrupt departures. "He told me I should take some time to deal with my family issues," Candido said. He collected his final paycheck a few days later.

*

While the kids were at school one afternoon, Candido and Brenda went to Dorothy's Place, a Catholic nonprofit based in Chinatown, Salinas's de facto

San Francisco City Hall forms the backdrop
to the homeless encampment put in place
during the Covid-19 pandemic.

skid row. With its block-long homeless encampments and open-air drug and prostitution market, the area seemed isolated and abandoned, designed to keep out any but the most desperate among the city's poor. For the couple, venturing there was a tacit admission that what they'd been going through could no longer be considered a brief setback. But it was immediately apparent that the services offered at Dorothy's Place were geared toward the single adults populating the streets outside the charity, not parents with kids. A case manager recommended that they try the Family Resource Center at Sherwood Elementary.

Founded in 2006, in the months leading up to the Great Recession, the resource center was the Salinas City Elementary School District's response to the growing problem of student home-lessness. Up to that point, the support available to homeless children and their families more or less consisted of Cheryl Camany, a teacher moonlighting part-time as the district's "homeless liaison," arranging the occasional shopping excur-sion to a discount department store. But suddenly Camany, who grew up in Salinas—her mom taught at Alisal High School, and her father owned a small grocery store called Camany's Market—was getting more requests for help. So she went around raising money from churches and businesses and persuaded the district's higher-ups to turn her liaison job into a full-time position.

At the same time, she began coordi-nating an effort to count the number of homeless students in each of the district's fourteen schools; in order to be helped, these children first needed to be identi-fied. That year, 261 students were discov-ered to be experiencing homelessness—a shocking figure, Camany thought. By

LIKE A MUSHROOM IN THE WOODS

There are plenty of strange accommodation options on Airbnb: a flying saucer in the UK, a "hotel" shaped like a potato in Idaho, wonderful treehouses all around the world to name just a few. Despite not standing out from the list, however, the best-loved of all is a cabin measuring just ten square metres in California. An hour-and-a-half's drive south of San Francisco, after venturing into the wooded slopes of the Santa Cruz Mountains and kissing goodbye to your phone signal, at a given point you come across a little wooden house topped by a geodesic dome: the famous Mushroom Dome. Built in the 1990s and listed on the short-term rentals site almost from the outset, it has been visited by around six thousand guests from more than forty countries. The highlight is its owner, the extraordinary Katherine Mrache – Kitty to her friends – a lady in her seventies who has lived in the woods since the 1980s and has no intention of leaving. Coming of age in the turbulent 1960s and having been immersed in the New Age spirituality of the later 20th century, her conversation alone makes the trek to the Mushroom Dome worth the effort. Another selling point is the much lower price than apartments in nearby San Francisco, which are now out of reach of the average tourist. Kitty's cabin embodies the more "idealist" spirit of Airbnb's origins, a company that wanted to enable those with a bit of space to earn some money without necessarily turning it into a business.

2012/13, the number was 2,042, and in every subsequent year it kept going higher. (Under the McKinney-Vento Act, every school district in the country is required to count and provide assistance to homeless students, but compliance is often spotty. In February 2019, California lawmakers announced a statewide audit to investigate why over four hundred school districts had failed to identify even a single homeless student.)

Brenda and Candido were nervous when they arrived at the Family Resource Center, which now occupied an entire building on Sherwood's campus and was run by four full-time staff members, Camany and three other women, all bilingual. "There was a lot of shame about our situation," Candido said. "We were always telling the kids, 'Don't be embarrassed. Don't feel bad.' But I guess we didn't follow our own advice. It seemed like we'd failed." Overcoming this stigma around the "H word," as Camany calls it, was an endless struggle at the resource center; there were many factors that kept families from seeking assistance—fear of referral to Child Protective Services or, in a place like Salinas, the undocumented status of some parents—but the humiliation of being homeless was perhaps the biggest one. "Sometimes the most therapeutic moment for the families we work with," Camany told me, "is when they realize how many others there are just like them."

Gradually, as Candido and Brenda started to feel more comfortable, the resource center became their lifeline. Camany and her colleagues wore many hats—social worker, therapist, financial adviser, surrogate mother—and the material assistance they provided was no less vital: the family was able to walk through a large adjacent room full of clothing, toiletries, backpacks, school supplies, sneakers, and bed linens, selecting anything they needed. They were given shower vouchers to use at a truck stop and gift cards for Safeway and McDonald's. The boys were enrolled in a free lunch and breakfast program called Second Opportunity Meals, and they began the process of setting up an Individualized Education Program for Josephat. A whole array of extracurricular activities, from the Youth Orchestra of Salinas to a nearby ranch where kids could learn to ride horses, was made available by partner organizations. They met people like themselves, parents who simply couldn't afford to keep their children housed. In the absence of this support, most of these families would have been left without a safety net of any kind, invisible to the system tasked with aiding them.

In late August 2019, Camany handed me the weekend edition of Salinas's newspaper, *The Californian*. She pointed to the headline—"Homeless Population Declines 15%"—then, shaking her head, she read aloud the finding that, according to the latest US Department of Housing and Urban Development-mandated Point-in-Time census, there were a mere 150 homeless families in the whole of Monterey County. (By contrast, according to the school data, there were 3,566 elementary-age homeless students in Salinas in 2018, or 40 per cent of the total student population.) As Camany observed, however, that low figure relied on a narrow—and, advocates argue, misleading—definition of homelessness used by HUD, which counts only those living on the streets or in shelters as "literally homeless." The Department of Education, on the other hand, widens the definition to include those living in cars, motels, or doubled up with others and accounts for the many reasons families might avoid a shelter or lack access to one.

> "She had come to recognize the signs of homelessness among her students without them having to say anything. When she spotted a kid hoarding snacks underneath his jacket, she brought him extra food the next day."

Yet it's HUD's definition that determines the allocation of crucial housing assistance. "It's a crazy logic," Barbara Duffield, the director of SchoolHouse Connection, a national youth-homelessness organization, told me. "It basically goes: *We don't see homeless families, so we don't have any here, therefore we don't have to help them.*"

One by one, these families appeared at the front door of the resource center, or called Camany on her ancient flip phone, or got sent her way by what she half-jokingly refers to as her network of "eyes and ears"—everyone from bus drivers to cafeteria workers. There was the young mom terrified of losing her eight-year-old son to the foster system because of persistent truancy. Camany promised to accompany her to the mediation session with the judge. There was the woman who arrived with a baby in her arms, sobbing uncontrollably. Diana Morales and Liliana Gil-Ramirez, two staff members, rushed to her side and stood embracing her for several minutes, whispering in Spanish; it turned out her husband, the family's breadwinner, had been arrested by ICE and was awaiting deportation.

Camany's ability to call attention to the scale and consequences of student homelessness had recently been paying off, and the mandate taken up by the resource center was being embraced by others: pastors and city leaders, school administrators and teachers. "There's so much injustice outside these walls," said Maria Castellanoz, a third-grade teacher,

Many of those camping out in Oakland and Salinas live in genuine poverty.

"but in my classroom, I make sure every student is treated with the dignity they deserve." Over time, she had come to recognize the signs of homelessness among her students without them having to say anything. When she spotted a kid hoarding snacks underneath his jacket, she brought him extra food the next day. When students nodded off in class, she let them sleep, tutoring them later so they wouldn't fall behind. All this had altered her understanding of what teaching should look like and what a school was for.

But there's only so much a school can offer. It can't give families apartments, or money, or jobs that pay a housing wage. It can't pass stronger tenant-protection laws or prevent exploitation by unscrupulous landlords. Oscar Ramos, who heads the elementary teachers' union, told me that he feared the long-term effects of such widespread volatility—that this "toxic stress," as pediatricians have termed it, would leave its mark on the physical and emotional health of his students well into the future (see "Toxic Stress" on page 40). "The more I learn about what these kids are carrying," Ramos said, "the more overwhelmed I get."

*

On my last night in Salinas I met Candido, Brenda, and the kids for dinner at Mountain Mike's Pizza on East Alisal Street. Unexpectedly, it would be something of a celebratory meal. Earlier that day, they'd received word that their application to rent a nearby house had been accepted. The Central Coast Center for Independent Living, a nonprofit focused on people with disabilities, had begun working with Brenda and determined that her increasingly debilitating condition made her eligible for rent assistance. The organization would be covering their security deposit, first month's rent, and a portion of the family's monthly rent of $2,600. Candido had also landed a new job cleaning recycling bins for the city, and he was now employed part-time as a custodian with the school district as well.

The kids were ecstatic as they jumped out of the minivan, yelling, "We got a house! We got a house!" Frankie and Josephat had been studying pictures of the two-bedroom house on Brenda's phone. They zoomed in on the room they'd be sharing, imagining where their bunk bed and toys would go. Their parents were beaming, too. "I told them not to get their hopes up," Candido said. "But yeah, we're pretty excited."

When the extra-large supreme pizza, the restaurant's "mountain" size, arrived at our table, the family looked at it tentatively, as if it could disappear. The past couple of days had been rough, Brenda said, nibbling at her salad. They couldn't spare the gas needed to drive to the mobile food bank located outside of town, so keeping themselves fed had been a challenge. After rationing throughout the week, all that remained at dinnertime the night before were four pieces of stale wheat bread and a can of Spam. Candido

TOXIC STRESS

When faced with danger, our bodies prepare us to respond to the threat by raising our heart rate, blood pressure and levels of stress hormones like cortisol. In children, when this response is triggered in a safe environment, the physiological effects are quickly turned off and return to normal, helping to develop a healthy stress-management system. However, if adverse events are prolonged or repeated, the physiological response is triggered but with no relief; over time the agents of stress destroy the existing neural connections and disrupt the creation of new ones, with lasting consequences on learning and behaviour as well as mental and physical health. This "toxic stress", mainly observed in conflict zones but also triggered by social factors – from socioeconomic status to discrimination – manifests itself in different ways: some children shake uncontrollably for hours, others become emotionally detached from the world and the people around them, others become anxious, frightened and/or aggressive. Some develop "resilience", or the ability to overcome severe difficulties – there are genetic and biological factors here, but studies suggest the most crucial thing is to have at least one stable and committed relationship with a parent or other adult. Other common factors that should be developed with effective therapy are a sense of self-efficacy and control over one's life, the ability to adapt and to practise self-control, to have sources of trust and hope and to have a sense of belonging to a cultural tradition.

and Brenda told the kids they weren't hungry and had them split the two sandwiches three ways. There had been lots of nights like that.

Frankie and Josephat inhaled their pizza and rushed off to a small cluster of arcade games, trailed by their sister. We watched as Frankie gingerly lifted his brother on to a bar stool so that he could reach the buttons; he stood behind Josephat, his hands poised near his younger brother's waist to keep him from falling. "That's Frankie," Candido said with a smile.

He went on to describe how advanced Frankie had been even at three or four: tying his own shoes, taking showers, reading books. Over the past two years, as Josephat's developmental delay grew more pronounced—"You can tell on his face that he's trying to communicate," Candido said, "but people don't understand him, and that's when he explodes in anger"—Frankie had been going out of his way to look after him. When Josephat's classmates started making fun of him, Frankie went to the boy's classroom every day to check on him; during recess, he would find his brother to make sure he wasn't sitting alone. Candido began to cry as he related this. "My son, he's eight years old," Candido said. "But he sees how stressed we are, how we're just trying to survive, and he puts that on himself. It's too much for a kid his age."

After dinner, I followed the family back to the parking lot where they'd been staying. The route took us along wide thoroughfares where a Denny's fast-food restaurant or an old auto shop would suddenly give way to brief stretches of farmland. To our left, the sunset made the shooting sprinkler water in a small broccoli field turn an iridescent orange. It was almost dark when we pulled into a municipal parking lot filled with row after row of white Ford Explorers. A security guard had told the family that they could no longer stay on hospital property, but he pointed them to an adjacent city lot overlooking the medical center. They now had to walk ten or fifteen minutes to use the ER bathroom, which was especially onerous when the kids were sick. Candido described a recent sleepless night of carrying Adelene, who had diarrhea, back and forth between the van and the hospital.

The children were already in their pajamas. In the back of the van Josephat had gone into what his parents said was his usual falling-asleep position: facedown, butt in the air, moaning softly, rocking back and forth. Adelene was in the front passenger seat, peeking out shyly between the seat and the raised headrest and clutching Addy, a giant stuffed cat named after her. Frankie was in his grizzly-bear sleeping bag, sitting up and facing Brenda, Candido, and me as we stood talking beside the van's open door. Earlier, at the restaurant, Brenda told me that at first Frankie had been claustrophobic in the van, but the sleeping bag, a present from his parents, put him at ease.

Unprompted, Frankie began telling us about a dream he'd had recently. It was the last day of school, and the teachers were letting the kids goof around in the hallways. Frankie and his friends were playing their favorite game, where some pretended to be zombies and the others, the zombie hunters, chased them with Nerf Blasters. "It was so much fun," he said drowsily. "There were special snacks, and we even got to watch a movie."

His mom asked him what it was like to wake up in the van.

"It felt really weird," he said. 🐦

Rematriation

For thousands of years before the arrival of Europeans, the territory we now know as California was inhabited and cared for by Indigenous people. After centuries of land grabs, genocide and environmental devastation, a movement calling for a return of the land to its legitimate custodians is finally achieving its first concrete results.

LAUREN MARKHAM
Photographs by Jana Ašenbrennerová

Members of the Costanoan Rumsen Carmel
tribe at the first Presidio Picnic of the year
at Presidio Park, San Francisco.

California's Palm Springs is known as a vacationers' paradise—a glam, mid-century modern Hollywood exurb draped in gilded light where crowds of golfing tourists, Los Angeles party people, and fashionable elders pass languid days in swimming pools and clink cocktails beneath the blistering desert sun. This Palm Springs traces its roots to the 1930s when Hollywood stars "discovered" it as an easy weekend getaway—an origin story that lends the place the sparkling allure of bygone days. But this place, like all places in California, has a long and often ignored history that has nothing to do with Hollywood.

In spring 2021, if you found yourself, as I did, heading to Palm Springs through the broad sweep of desert along Route 111, you'd have been offered up a more complete history lesson. Just as you entered town, you'd have seen it, the newest reminder of the place's oldest history, a row of massive white letters crafted in the same jaunty style as the iconic "Hollywood" sign: "INDIAN LAND."

Never Forget, as the installation was called, was created in the spring of 2021 by the artist Nicholas Galanin as a commission for the *Desert X* exhibition. The well-photographed sign, and its memory, served as a reminder that this place, and all the land in California and across the USA, was stewarded by Native communities for millennia before settlers came and is thus stolen land. This unavoidable fact is also one that has been long buried, cast aside and ignored by non-Native communities and those with political and economic power. But throughout California, and throughout the United States, this seems to be changing: conversations about the dispossession of and violence against Native tribes in the founding of this country and what might be owed as a result are beginning to enter more mainstream discourse. So, too, has a national movement to "rematriate" land gained traction—the notion of returning the land to the Indigenous communities from whom it was stolen long ago or restoring Mother Earth to her rightful caregivers.

The Land Back movement is a resistance movement, forms of which—large and small—have existed since settlers first arrived in what is now the United States, as Indigenous leaders refused to cede land or fought to keep construction off sacred landscapes. Today, Land Back isn't a single, centralized movement but an ethos, a slogan, a hashtag, and a demand that land be transferred back into Indigenous hands. This is a form of reparation for past wrongs that, a decade ago, was hardly discussed outside Indigenous and activist circles.

While land back movements have taken hold nationwide, some of the most substantial land transfers have occurred in California—a place with a particularly grisly history of theft, murder, and

LAUREN MARKHAM is a writer and journalist from Northern California whose work focuses on the environment, migration and California. Her book *The Far Away Brothers: Two Young Migrants and the Making of an American Life* was published by Crown in 2017, and her articles and reports have appeared in publications such as *VQR* (where she is a contributing editor), *Harper's*, *The New York Times Magazine*, the *Guardian*, *The New York Review of Books*, *The New Republic*, *Guernica*, *Freeman's*, *The Atlantic*, *The California Sunday Magazine*, *Zyzzyva* and numerous others. For many years she has also worked in the fields of education and immigration.

JANA AŠENBRENNEROVÁ is a Czech photojournalist and writer based in San Francisco who specialises in social documentary and portraiture. In collaboration with nonprofit organisations she documents humanitarian efforts all over the world. She has received numerous honours for her photography, including World Press Photo, National Geographic, China Press Photo, Czech Press Photo awards.

dispossession when it comes to Native peoples.

California—which, like all political entities with distinct borders, is an imaginary place that was for a long time called something else and something else still before that—is nothing if not a canvas for reinvention. "The future always looks good in the golden land," Joan Didion famously wrote of the state in *Slouching Toward Bethlehem*, "because no one remembers the past." Of course, she's referring only to white people—the Californians who have a particular stake in forgetting.

Europeans flocked to California on the promise of riches, yes, but for something much more than that: a chance to transform themselves, to leave the past behind in order to manifest an impossible future at the edge. (California, after all, stands at the rim of the continent; the place where the sun drops into the sea will always be seen as a place to chase dreams.) Today, people flock to Silicon Valley for many of the same reasons as they did during the Gold Rush: a chance to get rich and stake a claim in the newest empire. California, then, is an invented place that, for non-Indigenous people, has long been a canvas for personal dreams and the dreams of empire—and thus for erasure of the past.

The Land Back movement defies such erasure and asks that those with power—with political power, financial power, and land—face the wicked truth beneath California's gilded mythology and do something toward making it as right as possible. This, after all, as Galanin's sign insists we acknowledge and remember, is Indian Land.

"We live in a time of historical reconsideration," as Ojibwe writer David Treuer puts it in *The Atlantic* (May 2021), "as more and more people recognize that the sins of the past still haunt the present. For Native Americans, there can be no better remedy for the theft of land than land."

*

For thousands of years, Indigenous people lived in what is now known as California, living off and tending to the landscape. While the white imagination and history books have cast Native communities as primitive people, they lived in complex civilizations with elaborate roadways, political systems, foodways, and land-management practices. Prior to the European invasion, an estimated 300,000 people lived in California.

In the 1500s, the first Spanish "explorers" landed in what they christened "Alta California." By the 1700s, the Spanish had set up a network of Catholic missions snaking northward through the state. The missionaries forced Indigenous Californians to convert to Catholicism, leave their homes to live in the missions, and perform slave labor to keep the missions running. In many cases, children were separated from their families, and families were broken up and scattered in the name of "civilizing" the Indians. Settlers overhunted the wild game and introduced livestock that decimated the

INDIGENOUS CALIFORNIANS

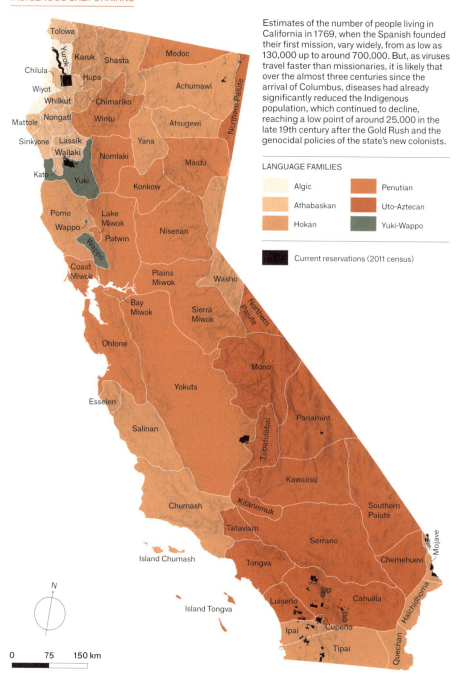

Estimates of the number of people living in California in 1769, when the Spanish founded their first mission, vary widely, from as low as 130,000 up to around 700,000. But, as viruses travel faster than missionaries, it is likely that over the almost three centuries since the arrival of Columbus, diseases had already significantly reduced the Indigenous population, which continued to decline, reaching a low point of around 25,000 in the late 19th century after the Gold Rush and the genocidal policies of the state's new colonists.

LANGUAGE FAMILIES
Algic
Athabaskan
Hokan
Penutian
Uto-Aztecan
Yuki-Wappo
Current reservations (2011 census)
Tolowa
Yurok
Karuk
Shasta
Modoc
Chilula
Hupa
Wiyot
Achumawi
Whilkut
Chimariko
Northern Paiute
Mattole
Nongatl
Wintu
Atsugewi
Sinkyone
Lassik
Yana
Wailaki
Nomlaki
Maidu
Kato
Yuki
Konkow
Pomo
Lake Miwok
Wappo
Patwin
Nisenan
Wappo
Coast Miwok
Plains Miwok
Washo
Bay Miwok
Sierra Miwok
Northern Paiute
Ohlone
Mono
Yokuts
Esselen
Panamint
Salinan
Tübatulabal
Kawaiisu
Chumash
Kitanemuk
Southern Paiute
Tataviam
Serrano
Mojave
Island Chumash
Tongva
Chemehuevi
N
Luiseño
Cahuilla
Island Tongva
Halchidhoma
Ipai
Cupeño
Tipai
Quechan
0
75
150 km

SOURCE: HANDBOOK OF NORTH AMERICAN INDIANS AND CAL OES

> "California, then, is an invented place that, for non-Indigenous people, has long been a canvas for personal dreams and the dreams of empire—and thus for erasure of the past."

ecosystem, leaving less food. Tens of thousands of Native Californians died during the mission period from lack of food, the wretched conditions of forced labor in the missions, from diseases such as smallpox to which the Native communities had little immunity, and because they were flat-out murdered (see "State Genocide" on page 48).

Then, in 1849, gold was discovered at Sutter's Mill in Northern California, sending out a siren call that drew people west with the promise of riches. That year alone, an estimated ninety thousand Europeans flooded California; in 1850, another hundred thousand Europeans arrived. On 9 September 1850, California was named the thirty-first state of the union. By this time, through settler violence and repression, there were only around seventy thousand Native Californians remaining in the state.

The more the population boomed, the more land, water, and other natural resources the settlers needed—and, as elsewhere, they saw the Native Californians as standing in their way. Civilians attacked, raped, and murdered Indians and stole their land from under them. Native Californians were forcibly removed off land their communities had been living on for centuries and then moved again and again. By 1887, 138 million acres (fifty-six million hectares) of California land was in the hands of Indigenous communities; by 1934, that area would dwindle to just forty-eight million acres (19.5 million hectares).

Meanwhile, military-run "reservations" were opened—essentially, concentration camps designed to control Native communities. My great-great-grandfather came to California in the mid-1800s and served as an army official whose job it was to guard one of these camps. Anyone of European ancestry who can trace their roots in California as far back as I can has a similar story of culpability and violence. The question is whether we choose to ignore the facts of our ancestors' sins or acknowledge them and do something about them.

Such an effort requires unlearning the tall tales we've been told, for I learned nothing of the aforementioned history growing up in San Francisco in the 1980s and 1990s. On the contrary, I learned that the missions were fascinating historical relics helping a population of "savages" adapt to the modern world. In the third grade, my class put on the annual California Pageant, a play in which each of us played a key character from Californian history. The performance began with the first missionary, Junipero Serra, walking onstage in a robe, making the sign of the cross, and proclaiming, "This is where I will build a mission." The history we were taught in our state back then is, in this way, one of complete erasure. "Inherent in the myth we've been taught," writes scholar Roxanne Dunbar-Ortiz in *An Indigenous Peoples' History of the United States* (Beacon Press, 2014), "is one of settler colonialism and genocide." Indeed, in my school and within my family, the pioneers were cast as my

The longstanding image of the early years of California as home to the Gold Rush and valiant pioneers has come under review, revealing a much darker picture than that in the textbooks of yore. Before it was even officially a state the California authorities instigated and financed raids targeting Indigenous populations, often disguised as expeditions against livestock rustlers, with the intent to commit genocide. Native Americans were targeted right across the state. The Round Valley, south-east of Yosemite, home to the Yuki people, suffered particularly heavily during a programme of genocide ordered in the 1850s by California's first chief justice, the landowner Serranus Hastings. A big name in the history of the San Francisco area, he founded the University of California's Hastings College of Law, alma mater of current US vice-president, Kamala Harris. There are many such instances in the state's history; the reputation of the founder of Stanford University is also sullied by crimes against Native Americans. But a recent revisiting of Hastings's biography shows that he ordered murderous expeditions of particular cruelty (one report describes a girl of ten killed "for obstinacy" and massacres of children) in an area where Indigenous people had been spared the earliest waves of colonisation. In response, the governing institutions of Hastings College began to consider how to make amends for this past, which, like any form of reparation, is a delicate operation, weighing what sort of compensation should be made and to whom. After months of deliberation the Law School announced it would change its name: we do not yet know what the new name will be, but the result has not satisfied some Native American leaders.

lauded forebears: quaint, brave people making their way with great hardship to build a vast new world—the very world in which I lived.

Much of this education persists today, but, in California at least, things are beginning, however slowly, to change. In 2017, the state rewrote its fourth-grade curriculum to do away with lessons that lionized the missions. And in July 2020, as part of the racial justice protests blooming throughout the United States, protestors forcibly toppled a statue of Junipero Serra that stood, imposing and grand, at the California State Capitol in Sacramento. Instead of rebuilding it, the capitol will erect a statue of Native Californians.

This realignment is long overdue. "To say that the United States is a colonialist settler-state," writes Dunbar-Ortiz, "is not to make an accusation but rather to face historical reality, without which consideration not much in US history makes sense, unless Indigenous people are erased." Indeed, much of what I learned growing up was an erasure story, as though Native Californians were a long-ago, primitive people who no longer lived among us, or lived at all, when in reality there are more than 700,000 native people who (despite every effort made to ignore the fact) reside in California today.

Facing these truths, can one see any other just path forward than to rematriate land into Indigenous hands?

*

In the spring of 2021, I met with Trina Cunningham, a community leader from the Mountain Maidu tribe, whose traditional lands spanned the lower Sierra Nevada mountains, to visit a recently rematriated parcel of land called Tásmam Koyóm (long known as Humbug

Alcatraz Island, Indian land.

In a commemoration held on Alcatraz Island to mark the fifty-second anniversary of its occupation (1969–71) by Indigenous demonstrators fighting for Native American rights, Shoshana Arai, from Tsuru for Solidarity, holds up a poster with an article and a collection of photographs about the protest dating from 1970.

such an intact landscape teeming with water and life.

But the landscape was more damaged than it might have seemed on first sight. In fact, Cunningham explained to me, to the Maidu's eyes, this landscape needed help. Instead of a wide wet marshland through which water flowed freely and widely, the meadow—through overgrazing by settler livestock—had become, effectively, a single central watercourse. That meant less biodiversity, more sediment flowing downstream, and a lower water table.

"Now that the land is ours again," Cunningham told me, "we can use the practices we've been using for millennia to care for this meadow and turn it healthy again."

Before it was transferred back into Maidu hands, this land was owned by the Pacific Gas and Electric Company (PG&E), a California utility that manages over half of the state's electricity grid, and a later

Valley—the name it was given on the map—by non-Indigenous).

Tásmam Koyóm is a broad mountain meadowland tucked into green conifer hills and fed by springs and snowmelt. It was beautiful—fresh water running through fields of blue-eyed grass and wildflowers where songbirds twittered and whirled through the brush. I'd driven four hours from where I lived in the city, having passed so many hillsides charred by wildfire, so it felt soothing to be in incarnation of what was once called the Great Western Power Company—a utility that, in the Gold Rush era, seized and thieved thousands of acres of land from Maidu communities in order to harness the Feather River's power. In 2001, the utility had to file for bankruptcy, and one of the terms of the bankruptcy agreement was to transfer large portions of the land they owned over for public use. The Maidu Summit Consortium, which Cunningham now runs, put in an application for the land.

First, they were told they didn't qualify because they weren't an official nonprofit organization. So they became a nonprofit. Then they were told they didn't qualify because they had no measurable history of land stewardship—in spite of their communities having lived in concert with and tended to the land for thousands of years before PG&E was even so named. But finally, over fifteen years later and after much hard work and fight, Tásmam Koyóm and five other parcels became theirs again.

"It's definitely a triumph," Cunningham told me. "It's been a long time coming."

Similar stories of rematriation are starting to bloom in California. In 2019, the city of Eureka—a verdant coastal town known for its towering redwoods and marijuana economy—made the decision to transfer two hundred acres (eighty-one hectares) of land to the Wiyot tribe. This land had been stolen from the Wiyot people following a brutal massacre in February 1860. Settlers murdered nearly two thousand Wiyot, sending only a few hundred survivors fleeing—families severed, land gone, generations of people haunted by this trauma.

"For our city," a Eureka city council-woman told the *Guardian* (21 October 2019), "it's the right thing to do, and that's

INDIGENOUS LANGUAGES UNDER THREAT

Uhyanapatánvaanich ("little word-asker"): this was the name given by the elders of the Karuk, a people of north-western California, to William Bright, the linguist who was welcomed into the community in 1949 to record their language, whose very few speakers were often reluctant to accept outsiders. After all, the mass extermination of Indigenous people had been accompanied by a system of enforced schooling in which young children, taken from their families and sent to institutions many miles away, lost contact with their land and their languages, leading them to forget and, worse, grow to be ashamed of their cultural and linguistic heritages. So many languages disappeared or were diminished in this way in California and with them aspects of the cultures they represented, cultures tightly bound to the ecosystems from which they emerged and which are themselves often also at risk. After studying Karuk, Bright was able to publish a dictionary with the help of the community, academic colleagues and the institutions that subsequently opened two bilingual schools teaching in both English and Karuk. Although still at risk, the language survives to this day. Bright's initiative was not an isolated one. In recent years at-risk languages in California have found help from their own last speakers – like Marie Wilcox, who devoted years of painstaking work to compiling a dictionary of Wukchumni in the hope of saving the language (which was then learned by her grandson), or Luther and Lucille Girado, whose conversations in Kawaiisu, of which they are the only remaining fluent speakers, have been recorded by Luther's daughter Julie to document the language and to ensure people can learn it even after Luther and Lucille are gone.

"To live in California today is to see the wreckage that land theft has wrought. Like the plunder of the human landscape, the European settlers from whom I am descended plundered the natural landscape, too."

why we're doing it. Certainly, it's been far too long."

In June 2020, the Esselen tribe of Monterey County purchased 1,200 acres (485 hectares) of their ancestral lands near central California's mountainous coast with financial support from the state of California and an Oregon conservation group. The land purchase will allow the tribe to carry out educational and community activities and spiritual ceremonies and would also ensure the protection of the fragile ecosystem. (If the tribe hadn't purchased it, it would have been split into five separate lots for residential or commercial development.) "We're the original stewards of the land," Esselen Tribal Chairman Tom Little Bear Nason told the *Santa Cruz Sentinel* in July 2020. "Now we're returned. We are going to conserve it and pass it on to our children and grandchildren and beyond."

I live in Berkeley, on the land of the Lisjan, or Ohlone, people, whose land and sacred sites were stripped from them. Like many smaller tribes, because the Ohlone people are not a federally recognized tribe—meaning they lack special designation by the US government—they remain, effectively, landless, which makes community organizing and cultural practices all the more difficult. Since the 1990s, a group of activists has been agitating to protect sacred sites, including the shellmounds where the Ohlone buried their dead (many of which have been paved over to build parking lots, roads, or shopping malls). In 2012, these activists launched the Sogorea Te' Land Trust in an effort to "reclaim traditional lands and reinstate cultural practices that became threatened under settlement." In 2017, another nonprofit transferred ownership of a quarter acre of land in Oakland to the Sogorea Te' Land Trust's hands—the first successful Land Back transfer in all of the East Bay region.

Walk around my West Berkeley neighborhood, and many people's windows or front yards are adorned with a "Give Shuumi" sign. This refers to the Shuumi land tax—a voluntary tax that non-Indigenous renters and homeowners like me can pay to the Land Trust in order to fund community activities and future land transfers, and, in a larger sense, to acknowledge what is owed and make a contribution to the people on whose land we outsiders are living. "Shuumi," explains Corinna Gould, co-founder of the Land Trust, "means a gift" in her native Chochenyo. Their website allows me to calculate the appropriate contribution: as a homeowner of a small two-bedroom house, the calculator tells me, I owe $300 per year. In 2018, the organization collected $80,000 of Shuumi from eight hundred separate contributors—a number that has only grown.

"It's your responsibility as settlers that come on to our land," Gould told a local radio program, "to actually give something back, and this is an easy way

The US secretary of the interior, Deb Haaland, the first Native American to hold that post, visits Alcatraz Island on the fifty-second anniversary of its occupation by Indigenous activists.

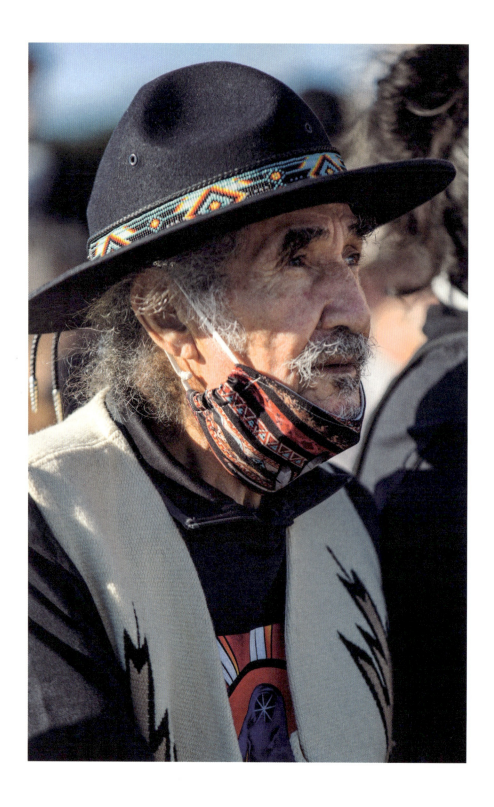

of doing that, a way for us to heal the horrific past that's not that long ago."

*

To live in California today is to see the wreckage that land theft has wrought. Like the plunder of the human landscape, the European settlers from whom I am descended plundered the natural landscape, too. Throughout much of the autumn our skies are choked with smoke. We can't make plans to spend time outside or travel for fear of fires or unbreathable air. Take a road trip, one of my favorite California pastimes (the open road is also a central part of our state's mythology), and you're bound to come across, often quite suddenly, a blackened swath of former forest—a landscape tarred and vanished by wildfire. You'll see, too, reservoirs so low they appear like puddles rather than stores of water, still-living forests that are desiccated and overgrown and thus all the more ready to burn. We've lost dozens of species of fish and birds and other wildlife, and many more—the tiger beetle, the delta smelt, the loggerhead sea turtle, the elf owl, the Sierra Nevada red fox—are endangered and risk being the next bit of California to be disappeared.

Even the California grizzly bear that stands tall and proud on our state's flag is now extinct.

Settler communities have been wretched stewards. The concept of private ownership rather than cooperative management and use is perhaps part of the problem. For in the realm of human history the mere concept of land ownership is relatively new; across the world, most Indigenous communities have always treated land as a sacred source of resources to be cared for and shared.

"We did not own the land, *we belonged to it*," writes Corinne Gould of Sogorea Te'. "Generation after generation, we cultivated reciprocal relationships with the plants and animals we shared this place with and developed beautiful and powerful cultural practices that kept us in balance."

The fate of the land is a fate we share—a fact that global Indigenous communities have been living by for millennia, and which is becoming more and more apparent to anyone attempting to disagree or wrest human control over a landscape. In California, where we live in a state of persistent drought and our wildfire season becomes longer and more brutal with each passing year, the stakes for a reimagined landscape are incredibly high. Land Back movements, then, aren't just a historical reparation—although they are certainly that—they are also a matter of returning Land Back into the hands of the people who know best how to care for it.

"Native people," writes Treuer, "need permanent, unencumbered access to our homelands—in order to strengthen us and our communities and to undo some of the damage of the preceding centuries." And the rest of us, just guests on this land, have a responsibility to pay what is owed. 🐦

Eloy Martinez, a veteran of the occupation of Alcatraz (1969–71) and a member of the Ute tribe, listens to the speech given by Deb Haaland, US secretary of the interior, during a visit to Alcatraz Island.

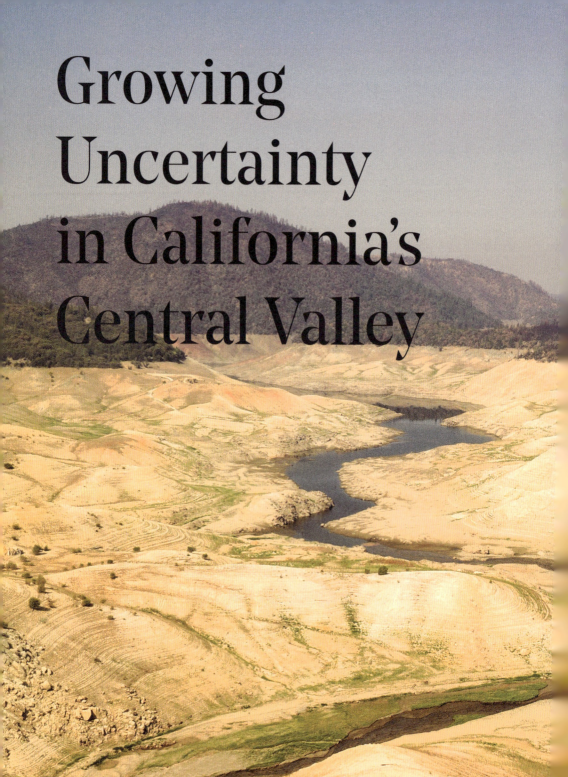

Growing Uncertainty in California's Central Valley

A bird's eye view over Lake Oroville in September 2021 when the lake was at only 23 per cent of full capacity following a period of extreme drought.

California produces much of the food that ends up on America's tables, but with increasingly regular and longer droughts and frequent interruptions to the supply chain, it is time to ask whether the current system is sustainable.

ANNA WIENER
Photographs by Josh Edelson

57

One weekend in late June, I drove with friends to Yolo County, California, a rural area in the Sacramento Valley. It was the second day of a multiday heatwave, and temperatures approached the triple digits Fahrenheit. The road shimmered. In the passenger seat, a friend, seven months pregnant, wondered aloud whether it was safe for her to be outside. As we neared our destination, winding through fruit and nut farms, we passed a walnut orchard. Its trees had been cut down to the roots—the trunks neatly dominoed, flat and brittle against the earth.

That night, I asked a farmer friend, also in walnuts, what had happened at the orchard. A confluence of things, he explained. Walnuts are a billion-dollar industry, but during the pandemic things got complicated. In California, there was an ongoing labor crisis; also, owing to global supply-chain upsets, the costs of machinery and mechanical parts had gone up. My friend guessed that the orchard I had seen would still have been productive for another decade, but it no longer made financial sense to farm and harvest it.

Across the state, he said, many produce farmers were weighing the market prices of their crops against the rising cost of water. To meet their contracts, some had overplanted, and now they found it was more cost-effective to kill certain crops than to proceed with the harvest. Others had already scaled back and planted less. Farmers were throttling production, razing fields, and disposing of surplus. If these adjustments seemed crude, even unfathomable, they were in response to complex, intertwined issues: immigration policies, trade wars, a housing shortage, agribusiness monopolies, resource mismanagement, climate change, globalization, supply-chain disruption, accelerating financialization.

"It's like something out of a Jonathan Franzen novel," I said. My friend misheard. "Really?" he replied. "I'd love to read that."

*

California went through an extreme drought in 2021, after a decade marked by record-breaking dry spells. Rivers and reservoirs were low and strained. Aquifers drained; wells dried up. Some households didn't have access to clean water, whereas others were rationed for months. This led to a great many uses of the word "emergency": a drought state of emergency was declared for 42 per cent of the state's residents; an emergency

ANNA WIENER grew up in Brooklyn and moved to San Francisco in 2013 to work in the tech sector. Her experiences in that world, and her disillusion with it, led to her writing a memoir, *Uncanny Valley* (MCD, 2020, USA / Fourth Estate, 2020, UK), which was an international success. She is a contributing editor to *The New Yorker* focusing mainly on Silicon Valley, the world of startups and technology, and has written for *n+1*, *The Atlantic* and *The New Republic*.

CORIANDER / CILANTRO

One crop that has expanded hugely in recent years, although still remaining far less important than alfalfa, is coriander/cilantro (depending where you come from): in 2019 over 42,000 tonnes were produced, almost double the figure of 25,000 in 2006. Grown mainly in Monterey and Ventura counties, the herb requires moderate temperatures to thrive – otherwise it will flower too quickly and produce few leaves – but it grows year-round and is thus used in crop rotations. For the same reason, in some years growers decide to double their earnings by taking in more than one harvest. But, above all, the boom has come about following a strong growth in demand: in the last decade not only has the Golden State seen significant growth – by 11 and 25 per cent respectively – in its Latino and Asian populations, whose recipes frequently call for the leaves, but it also seems that consumers of all stripes are starting to add it to their dishes. But not everyone's a fan: in fact, the population seems to be split between those who love it and those who just cannot stand it, with almost all its detractors saying it leaves them with a soapy taste in their mouths. This alignment of tastes is no coincidence: scientists have reportedly discovered a sensory receptor associated with a particular gene (OR6A2) that reacts in the presence of certain organic compounds present in the herb, communicating the presence of an unpleasant taste to the brain. So lovers of coriander or cilantro (whichever name you call it by) are born rather than made.

curtailment order prohibited further depletion of the Sacramento-San Joaquin Delta watershed; in an emergency procedure, nearly seventeen million juvenile Chinook salmon, spawned in Central Valley hatcheries, were displaced by truck to deeper, cooler bodies of water. In May 2021, farmers with ties to right-wing activist Ammon Bundy camped along the border with Oregon to protest water shut-offs. In August that year, the federal government declared a water shortage for the Colorado River, which, among other crucial functions, feeds Lake Mead, the reservoir propelling the Hoover Dam—a significant source of power for Nevada, Arizona, and Southern California. Lake Oroville can no longer support its underground hydroelectric plant. Illegal cannabis growers are thought to be conducting overnight water heists. Governor Gavin Newsom, who in September 2021 won a recall election that threatened to remove him from office, has asked Californians to reduce their personal water usage by 15 per cent. This isn't the first such request, and people know what to do: they neglect the lawn, skip the car wash, watch the tap, and line the bathtub with buckets for gray water. Before I lived in California, I used to find Joan Didion's rhapsodic appreciation of municipal waterworks in her 1977 essay "Holy Water"—"The water I will draw tomorrow from my tap in Malibu is today crossing the Mojave Desert from the Colorado River, and I like to think about exactly where that water is"—a little unconvincing. It seemed like poetic license. Now I see that it is the sentiment of someone for whom basic infrastructure has proved unreliable.

Lifestyle adjustments help, but 80 per cent of water usage in California is agricultural. Almonds are famously water-intensive and so is alfalfa, a top agricultural commodity for California and a preferred feed among livestock handlers. In an arrangement of synchronicity known as the dairy–forage continuum, alfalfa, "the queen of forages," is one of the state's highest-acreage crops, and California is the leading dairy producer in the United States: nearly two million dairy cows loiter about, chewing. California exports about 15 per cent of its alfalfa to markets in China, Saudi Arabia, South Korea, Japan, and the United Arab Emirates—areas where demand for dairy products is rising. In the 2010s, the cultivation of animal-feed grasses was banned in Saudi Arabia, owing to unsustainable water consumption, and Almarai, a multinational dairy company based there, purchased thousands of acres of farmland in California and Arizona and used them to grow alfalfa. Foreign investment in California farmland is not new—international firms, many British, own more than a million acres (nearly half a million hectares)—but the cultivation of a water-intensive crop in a drought-addled state has proved controversial: "We're not getting oil for free, so why are we giving our water away for free?" an Arizona county politician once asked.

I first read about alfalfa after seeing the razed walnut orchard. I wanted to know how the place where I live was changing. Over the past few years, various crises have emerged or accelerated in California, and on trips across the state, particularly in the summer months, I have felt an acute sense of foreboding. An ongoing experience of ambient instability was not useful; getting into specifics offered some structure. There was plenty to read—about the globalization of farmland, the connections between milk and alfalfa, cows and oil. It reminded me of a joke. Two cows are in a field. One cow says to the other, "Hey, are you worried about that mad-cow disease?" The other cow shakes her head. "Mad-cow disease?" she asks. "I'm a helicopter."

*

Most investigations into California agriculture begin with the Central Valley: a depression, largely bounded by mountain ranges, that spans much of the state and is responsible for more than a third of the country's vegetables and two-thirds of its fruits and nuts. The region's growers provide almost all the celery, garlic, figs, olives, raisins, kiwis, and canning tomatoes in the United States and also the varieties of tree nuts that one might purchase at a gas station: pistachios, almonds, pecans, walnuts.

The plenitude of the Central Valley is a point of pride for many Californians, but it is a frightening one to encounter for the first time in the summer of 2021, following the world's hottest month on record and the Intergovernmental Panel on Climate Change's latest report. ("Two-thirds?" a friend in New York gasped recently, after generously indulging a monologue on alfalfa. "That's a terrible idea!") For years, academics and others have pointed out that California's current agricultural industry is unsustainable and long overdue for either a reckoning or a restructuring. Some argue that the solution lies in sustainable farming, practiced by small and midsize farms growing a diversity of crops—but for now federal farm policy tends to favor larger, industrial operations, many of them in the business of monocropping. In *Perilous Bounty: The Looming Collapse of American Farming and How We Can Prevent It*, published by Bloomsbury in 2020 and written before the pandemic,

The Domaine Carneros winery
in Napa Valley.

Tom Philpott, a journalist for the progressive magazine *Mother Jones*, suggests that produce farming should be decentralized and that California agriculture should be scaled back to adapt to its water resources. The future of the Central Valley, Philpott argues, is increasingly imperiled, and it is untenable to rely on the region for such a significant portion of the country's food.

Most consumers only ever experience the end points of supply chains, but the pandemic has offered a glimpse of the contingencies and vulnerabilities of California's food systems. The phrase "supply chain" is something of a misnomer. The reality is something closer to a network or web than an assembly line or a Rube Goldberg/Heath Robinson machine. Supply and demand are enmeshed with manufacturing, shipping, logistics, storage, warehousing, and distribution, and with retail trends, economic policy, international relations, immigration, digital marketplaces, climate change, and public health. The pandemic was a shock to the network; it snarled the web.

In May 2020, the *Los Angeles Times*

Above: An abandoned boat on a dried-up section of Lake Oroville.
Opposite top: Activists from the Last Chance Alliance call on Governor Gavin Newsom to work to eliminate the use of fossil fuels and help tackle the climate emergency in California.
Opposite bottom: Workers at the Christopher Ranch in Gilroy work on the garlic production line. The local garlic industry benefited from US trade sanctions on China.

ran an article with the headline "Skip the Steak, Buy the Brisket: Consumers Need to Be Flexible Amid Beef Bottlenecks." Beef production—the slaughtering of cattle and the packaging of beef—had dropped by nearly 40 per cent nationally since the start of the pandemic. Producers, who purchase cattle from ranchers, had stopped buying; some ranchers put their animals up for auction; retail prices rose, and a backlog of live animals meant tanking prices for cattle. The bottleneck was that workers in some slaughterhouses and packing plants were contracting Covid-19 and dying. Although farm and factory workers were deemed essential, their employers often failed to provide adequate PPE, barriers, or information about outbreaks; some workers were in the US on short-term agricultural visas and lived in tightly packed, employer-provided dormitories. A few months into the pandemic, agricultural counties in California had developed some of the highest per-capita Covid rates in the state. That July, *T: The New York Times Style Magazine* published an article on Americans' embrace of comfort food, headlined "What We Eat During a Plague." It ran with a highly stylized photograph of an antique plaster bust, wreathed in greens and raw brisket.

Other supply-chain problems were rooted in the pre-pandemic world. California is one of the world's largest producers of so-called processing tomatoes, fruits that are thick-skinned and durable, harvested mechanically, and sold for downstream use. Historically, the export market for them has been robust, but in recent years the strength of the dollar has made many American products too expensive for international consumers, and so demand for American tomato products began to wane. Tomato

SALTON SEA

California's largest lake formed in 1905 when flooding caused the waters of the Colorado River to flow into a depression in the middle of the desert. The area became a well-known tourist destination for the wealthiest Californians, an inland sea surrounded by villas, resorts and golf courses. Everything started to change in the 1970s, however, when a series of floods devastated some of the facilities. By this point the lake was fed only by the run-off from the intensively cultivated fields of the surrounding area, full of fertilisers and pesticides. Levels of salinity, caused by deposits on the lake bed, went up, which led to a gradual increase in the concentration of algae. The waters became oxygen depleted and began to retreat, a process that is ongoing. The ecosystem is now uninhabitable for a great many fish species, and fish bones and other skeletons accumulate on the banks, while the fish that do survive are harmful to the migratory birds that visit the Salton Sea. And the lake is also a threat to the health of local people. As the waters have receded they have revealed a lake bed impregnated with poisons. As the bed dries out in the sun a "toxic dust" forms, which is picked up and carried by the wind, along with the stench, causing respiratory diseases in humans, with asthma rates extremely high. But a community of anarchists, artists and marginalised people has also sprung up around the lake, living among the ruins of a military base. This is Slab City, a post-apocalyptic settlement combining refuse and dereliction with new life, sometimes with impressive results – like Salvation Mountain, a vast mound of recycled materials that rises up in the middle of the desert painted in gaudy colours and dedicated to Christian salvation.

processors started putting in smaller orders, and some growers responded by shifting away from tomatoes and toward higher-value crops, such as pistachios, almonds, and olives. Meanwhile, steel tariffs imposed by the US in 2018 led to a shortage of steel sheets, which are used to make food cans, and production costs soared; processing plants across California closed. All this meant that even before the pandemic there were already fewer processed-tomato products than usual. When Covid arrived and consumers hoarded shelf-stable, processed tomatoes—salsa, ketchup, sauce; cubed, diced, peeled—tomato processors scrambled to divert their food-service supply chains (gallon jugs meant for restaurants and institutional kitchens) to retail manufacturing (tiny bottles meant for pantries). Prices, which had already been rising, continued to climb. The drought of 2021 is expected to cause shortages and escalating prices as we move through 2022.

In other cases, the pandemic dovetailed with climate change. The rise of Covid coincided with the 2020 Dungeness crab season; early that year, China, a major export market for Dungeness crabs, banned live-animal imports. Then, as the virus spread in the USA, restaurants closed and demand for fresh crab plummeted. Wholesalers, to which most fishermen sell their catch, froze the surplus; some launched direct-to-consumer e-commerce sites. Later that year, when another season rolled around, rising ocean temperatures pushed anchovies into California's coastal waters, and about 350 whales followed in pursuit. Large fishing nets threatened to entangle the whales, and so the fishing season for crab was delayed until they dispersed. When the whales finally left, in late December, Pacific Seafood, a major West Coast wholesaler, announced that it would be offering an unusually low price for Dungeness crab because the company still had plenty frozen from the previous year's catch; this resulted in a sort of unilateral strike among fishermen, although they have no formal union.

For some farms, of course, the pandemic created new and occasionally lucrative opportunities. Smaller farms, such as those specializing in organic or heirloom produce, could be nimble. Some created farm-box and Community Supported Agriculture programs; others launched e-commerce sites or worked with regional grocery-delivery companies. Early on in the pandemic, I began picking up farm-boxes offered by an organic farmer with land in the Salinas Valley who had sold directly to Bay Area restaurants for the past thirty years. Some weeks, the cardboard box contained items that I had never seen before: sudachi, cardoons, flowering coriander. It seemed vaguely immoral, or at least absurd, that my household was eating better than ever before.

*

What's the upshot of all this turbulence? Oddly, 2020 was a decent year for California agriculture. In certain cases, federal subsidies padded the fallout; government purchases for food banks and assistance programs helped sustain struggling industries. In 2021, the industry saw record demand for beef and almonds. Gradually, restaurants reopened, Dungeness crabs repopulated fishmongers' tanks, and tomatoes returned to the shelves. Disruptions can have long half-lives: price changes for consumers represent material changes for the hundreds of thousands of people whose livelihoods depend on California's agricultural economy. Still, California's food systems are adaptable. The industry's economic strength can be difficult to reconcile with the social, political, and ecological challenges up ahead.

The Central Valley's abundance has long been attributed to its Mediterranean climate—a comparison which belies the reality that the climate of the actual Mediterranean is changing. The California drought of 2021 was so severe that to offset it will require a string of wet years in a row. But rain is only part of the equation. Rising temperatures dry out the soil; wildfires, per a May 2021 report in *Sierra Club* magazine, "Fire Season's Impact on Our Water," alter "the land's ability to self-regulate." In a 2018 paper, "Climate Change Trends and Impacts on California Agriculture: A Detailed Review," published in the journal *Agronomy*, researchers in the University of California system concluded that the state's climate had changed so significantly that urgent adaptation was needed in the agricultural sector to address a number of accelerating negative trends, including "crop yield declines, increased pest and disease pressure, increased crop water demands ... and uncertain future sustainability of some highly vulnerable crops." In his book, Tom Philpott of *Mother Jones* details the Great Flood of 1861–2, which blanketed the Central Valley in more than ten feet (three meters) of water; the United States Geological Survey, he notes, has conducted research on the likelihood of another, similarly devastating megastorm in this century, which would decimate—and drown—the region. (Reading this, I thought of my friend's exclamation: "Two-thirds?")

During the unprecedented and prolonged heat of the summer of 2021, California farmworkers, exposed to triple-digit Fahrenheit temperatures, were vulnerable to dehydration and heatstroke. Dairy cows suffered from heat stress, and steers and lambs were lethargic. Prune plums dropped prematurely; tree nuts and apples were sunburned. Up the coast, in Canada and the Pacific Northwest, berries rotted on the vine, baby hawks jumped their nests to avoid the sun, and clams and mussels baked in their shells. Avocados and lemons are smaller than usual. Food staples are getting more expensive. Smaller short-grain-rice plantings in the Sacramento Valley, coupled with a looming salmon shortage, portend a crisis for the "sushi supply chain." Meanwhile, if the past few fire seasons are any indication, farmworkers will continue to pick produce in ash-laden air, harvesting fields thick with smoke for the fifth year in a row.

Global trade networks, already disrupted by the pandemic, have also been affected by extreme weather: in July 2021, an enormous typhoon shuttered ports across eastern China. Coronavirus outbreaks in Vietnam and Bangladesh caused factory shutdowns. A natural-rubber shortage seemed imminent, following China's stockpiling the material for its national reserves, fungal leaf disease in Sri Lanka, and drought and floods in Thailand and Indonesia. There have been delays for farm machinery and for essential components such as box blades, microchips, plastics, pallets, and the foam required for tractor seats. The cost of steel spiked. Fertilizer prices soared, owing to tariffs, rising energy and freight costs, and a surge in demand following intense weather in some regions. Port delays caused agricultural exporters to be anxious about fruit decay, and airlines, capitalizing on the congestion, chartered passenger planes to fill their seats with high-value freight. Dozens of container ships were anchored off the coast of Southern California, packed with imports and waiting to unload. Extreme weather and Covid outbreaks shut down ports and airports in Asia.

Change is inevitable; it's less certain what will change first, whom it will benefit, and at what cost. Farmland owners are turning toward renewable energy, converting vegetable fields to acres of solar panels; Amazon and Costco have built warehouses in the Central Valley. There is growing competition from Mexican farms; a seven-year study has found favorable conditions for almond-growing in Idaho. The average age of California farmers is fifty-nine years old, and in the near future nearly four hundred million acres (160 million hectares) of agricultural land across the country is expected to change hands. Since the mid-2000s, farmland has become an appealing asset class, with private-equity firms and other institutional investors—Prudential and UBS among them—buying up agricultural properties, which poses a threat to younger farmers who aspire to someday own and cultivate their own plots of land.

As a finite resource, farmland is expected to appreciate over time, especially in the context of a growing population with growing needs for food, fiber, and fuel. In the book *Fields of Gold: Financing the Global Land Rush* (Cornell University Press, 2020), Madeleine Fairbairn attributes the current financial interest in farmland to the 1980s, when agricultural-commodity-derivative markets were deregulated and inundated with capital; the financial crisis of 2008, along with that year's food crisis, was a "tipping point." The phenomenon,

THE AGRICULTURAL EMPIRE

While they were recently overtaken by Bill Gates – who, with 242,000 hectares, became the largest owner of agricultural land in the USA in 2020 – with the 190,000 hectares controlled by the Wonderful Company, Stewart and Lynda Resnick remain the sector leaders, ruling over California in almost feudal style. Their fiefdom is the San Joaquin Valley, where their most important crops are almonds, pistachios, grapes, mandarins and pomegranates. When it comes to nuts, they have a quasi-monopoly, adjusting prices as they see fit and exploiting every kind of public or private water resource to irrigate crops requiring vast quantities of water, the most controversial aspect of their business. One journalistic investigation revealed that in Kern County, Wonderful had built a secret pipeline illegally taking water from the area's farmers. Because his orchards are so thirsty, Stewart Resnick even reached agreements with his former enemy John Vidovich, a businessman who specialises in taking possession of water-rich land and selling it on. Lynda Resnick is regarded as the brains behind the company's marketing strategies, presenting Wonderful's products as superfoods and associating them with a healthy lifestyle (the company has been found guilty of misleading advertising), as well as its image-glossing PR campaigns that rely on a network of contacts within the jet set and highlighting its major philanthropic projects – notably Lost Hills, a town effectively owned by the couple, where they provide work for three in every four residents and have built houses, schools, parks and restaurants. Wonderful stands out for its good practice in terms of pay policy, however; back in 2019 it introduced a minimum hourly wage of $15, which has, since 2022, been applied at state level.

Above: Customers shopping at a farmer's market in San Rafael.
During the pandemic many residents started visiting markets to avoid
the confined spaces of large stores and to support local farmers.
Above right: Boats moored in a much-reduced Lake Oroville.
Opposite: An empty water tank in East Porterville. The town ran out
of water, forcing residents to look elsewhere for supplies.

THE PASSENGER   Anna Wiener

While in the grip of a severe drought in 1991, San Diego imposed a 30 per cent reduction in the consumption of water resources. The restriction hit residents and the local economy, which is notable for its biotechnology industry, as scientists could no longer clean their laboratory equipment. The city learned from that experience and now sets an example that bucks the trend in the rest of California with water reserves that can shield it even from periods of the most severe drought. The successful strategy is based on a mix of factors: a culture of water-saving and awareness-raising aimed at residents but, above all, diversification. In 1996 San Diego began sourcing water from the Imperial Valley in addition to the Colorado River, lining the canals with concrete to prevent the water soaking into the ground. In 2014 the San Vicente Dam was built, creating a huge reservoir near the city. The following year a desalination plant was inaugurated, although it became the focus of much controversy because of the huge costs and its massive energy consumption. To make it drinkable, ocean water has to be forced through a very fine membrane at high pressure, expending huge amounts of energy, energy that is not produced from renewable sources. Pumping water from the ocean and discharging the highly saline residue from the process back into the marine environment also damages the ecosystem. Yet, while in 2015 desalination was seen as a resource only in times of extreme necessity, it is now welcomed as the salvation of San Diego's water resources. The cost of "the world's most expensive drinking water", as it has been dubbed, seems to have become acceptable.

she argues, is "the result of cumulative changes, including the professional farm-management capacity acquired in the aftermath of past booms and busts, as well as institutional investors' ever-expanding search for new ways to deploy their swelling pools of capital": if you have billions to protect, farmland might help you stay ahead of inflation. (As of 2020, Bill and Melinda Gates are the largest private farmland owners in the country.) Hedge-fund managers are eyeing water rights in Arizona and Colorado; Harvard's endowment fund has moved into vineyards; there is a futures market for California water. The time horizon for investments is rarely calculated on an ecological scale. Barring disaster or government intervention, California agriculture will remain an attractive place to park some capital for a while to come.

*

Nine days after my trip to Yolo County, I travelled from San Francisco to Sequoia National Park. The five-hour drive cut through the Central Valley. On the way, the fields were a patchwork, some irrigated and abundant, others parched and ochre. The heat was heavy and dry.

Wildfire season had already begun, and, as the car pitched along the road through Kings Canyon, I tried to tamp down a feeling like dread. In California, where the effects of global warming are pervasive and unsubtle, spending time in the forest always makes me feel unspeakably lucky and dizzy with remorse. Families in masks stomped through the Giant Forest to pose for photographs in front of General Sherman, a 275-foot-tall (84-meter) tree (see "Super Trees" on page 110). Children licked ice-cream bars by the visitor center. In the parking lot, some of the oldest living trees in the world shaded eight-seat SUVs: Kia Tellurides, Chevy Tahoes, Toyota Sequoias.

The next day, my companion and I hiked down a trail, which we had spotted from the road, that led to the Kings River at the bottom of the canyon. It was a path of quick switchbacks and seemingly intended for fishermen. The trail was overgrown and exposed, a foolish place to be in the late-morning sun, and we had not packed enough drinking water. Instead, my backpack held a bathing suit, two oatmeal cookies, and a copy of Sally Rooney's *Beautiful World, Where Are You* (Farrar, Straus and Giroux, USA / Faber and Faber, UK, 2021). In the book, a character has a moment of sociopolitical clarity while standing in a market: "This is it, the culmination of all the labour in the world, all the burning of fossil fuels and all the back-breaking work on coffee farms and sugar plantations," she frets, eyeing the chips, the sodas, the packaged foods. "All for this! This convenience shop!" This is good material for fiction; with minimal shorthand, it exposes the world as improbable, a sequence of fragile contingencies, while communicating something about a character's political affinities and her sense of implication.

As we hiked down to the river, I thought about other novels in which characters experience their own supply-chain revelations: brief, dissociative, quasi-psychedelic confrontations with retail-level commodities. In an oft-cited passage in Ben Lerner's novel *10:04* (Picador, 2014, USA / Granta, 2015, UK), the narrator experiences one as he stands in a scavenged Manhattan Whole Foods on the eve of Hurricane Irene's landfall: "It was as if the social relations that produced the object in my hand began to glow within it as they were threatened, stirred inside their packaging, lending it a certain aura—the majesty and murderous stupidity of that organization of time and space and fuel and labor becoming visible in the commodity itself now that planes were grounded and the highways were starting to close." In Benjamin Kunkel's *Indecision* (Random House, 2005), a character, high out of her gourd, fantasizes about a magical fruit that bestows the power of supply-chain transparency. "When you eat from this fruit then whenever you put your hand on a product, a commodity, an article, then, at the moment of your touch, how this commodity came into your hands becomes plainly evident to you," she explains. "Now there is no more mystification of labor, no more of a world in which the object arrives by magic—scrubbed, clean, no past, all of its history washed away."

Spending time in the sequoia groves—peaceful, resourced, ancient, maintained—had temporarily lulled me into a state of climate amnesia. But by the time we reached the river the temperature was in the nineties Fahrenheit. We drank carefully, titrating water from plastic cycling bottles, mouthing the caps like gerbils. There was no magic, no psychedelic insight into social relations, no sense of revelation—only the faint sensation that the land was changing in severe and irreparable ways and might, in my own lifetime, grow unfamiliar, unreliable. The banks were empty. The current was strong, and the river looked low. For a few minutes, we sat in the shade. ✒

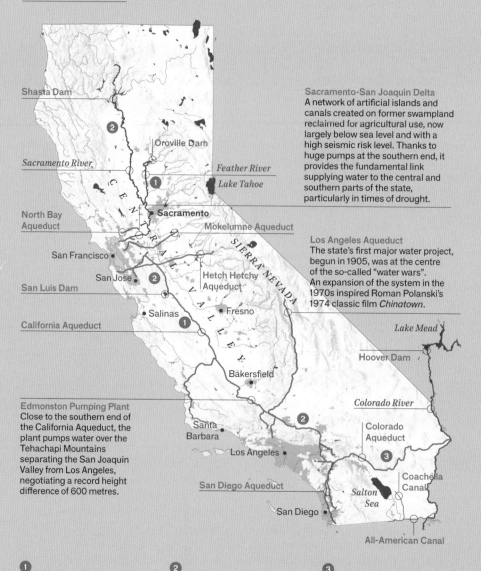

Shasta Dam

Oroville Dam

Sacramento River

Feather River

Lake Tahoe

North Bay Aqueduct

● **Sacramento**

Mokelumne Aqueduct

San Francisco ●

San Jose ●

San Luis Dam

Hetch Hetchy Aqueduct

● Salinas

● Fresno

California Aqueduct

SIERRA NEVADA

CENTRAL VALLEY

Bakersfield

Lake Mead

Hoover Dam

Colorado River

Colorado Aqueduct

Santa Barbara

Los Angeles ●

Coachella Canal

San Diego Aqueduct

Salton Sea

San Diego ●

All-American Canal

Sacramento-San Joaquin Delta
A network of artificial islands and canals created on former swampland reclaimed for agricultural use, now largely below sea level and with a high seismic risk level. Thanks to huge pumps at the southern end, it provides the fundamental link supplying water to the central and southern parts of the state, particularly in times of drought.

Los Angeles Aqueduct
The state's first major water project, begun in 1905, was at the centre of the so-called "water wars". An expansion of the system in the 1970s inspired Roman Polanski's 1974 classic film *Chinatown*.

Edmonston Pumping Plant
Close to the southern end of the California Aqueduct, the plant pumps water over the Tehachapi Mountains separating the San Joaquin Valley from Los Angeles, negotiating a record height difference of 600 metres.

❶
CENTRAL VALLEY PROJECT (CVP)
A federal project begun during the New Deal era of the 1930s, water is transported from the Sacramento River through the Sacramento-San Joaquin Delta to the San Joaquin Valley.

SOURCE: WIKIPEDIA

❷
STATE WATER PROJECT (SWP)
The largest water-management system in the USA, the state-run SWP was initiated in the 1960s. The system transports water from Lake Oroville, an artificial reservoir, to Los Angeles (a ten-day trip) through the California Aqueduct and other canals, some of them shared with the CVP.

❸
COLORADO RIVER SYSTEMS
The waters of the Colorado River, managed through Lake Mead, which was formed by the Hoover Dam (1935), are another important source of supplies for the south of the state, but they are shared with six other states as well as Mexico and considered overexploited, particularly by California.

The growth of California has depended to a large extent on its ability to manage its scarcest – and most precious – resource: water. In a normal year a third of the water used by the state comes from groundwater and the rest comes from the rivers. This surface river water has to be stored and distributed, because most of it (75 per cent) is located to the north of Sacramento where rainfall is abundant, whereas 80 per cent of the demand lies to the south of the capital. These imbalances have been resolved in part by the construction of one of the world's most sophisticated water-storage-and-transportation systems, an integrated network of dams, reservoirs, pumps and aqueducts under federal, state and private ownership that transport water from the mountains to the coast and from north to south. But years of drought have reignited the debate over who has the rights to the ever-scarcer water resources, and the entire system is being called into question, to the extent that those lucky enough to be sitting on water deposits that have yet to dry up are better off selling the water than using it, and the growers of thirsty crops, like the state's lucrative almonds, prefer to leave the trees to die – and replace them with solar panels.

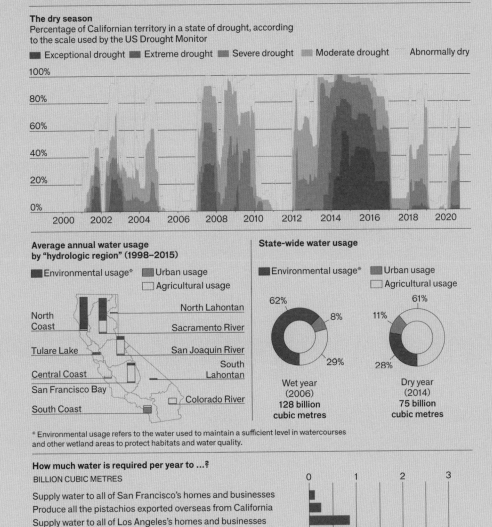

The dry season
Percentage of Californian territory in a state of drought, according to the scale used by the US Drought Monitor

- Exceptional drought
- Extreme drought
- Severe drought
- Moderate drought
- Abnormally dry

Average annual water usage by "hydrologic region" (1998–2015)

- Environmental usage*
- Urban usage
- Agricultural usage

North Coast
North Lahontan
Sacramento River
Tulare Lake
San Joaquin River
Central Coast
South Lahontan
San Francisco Bay
Colorado River
South Coast

State-wide water usage

- Environmental usage*
- Urban usage
- Agricultural usage

62%
8%
29%

Wet year (2006)
128 billion cubic metres

11%
61%
28%

Dry year (2014)
75 billion cubic metres

* Environmental usage refers to the water used to maintain a sufficient level in watercourses and other wetland areas to protect habitats and water quality.

How much water is required per year to …?
BILLION CUBIC METRES

Supply water to all of San Francisco's homes and businesses
Produce all the pistachios exported overseas from California
Supply water to all of Los Angeles's homes and businesses
Produce all the walnuts exported overseas from California
Produce all the almonds exported overseas from California
Produce all California's almonds

SOURCE: US DROUGHT MONITOR, PUBLIC POLICY INSTITUTE OF CALIFORNIA, MOTHER JONES

What Does It Mean to Be a Solution?

The Asian-American community is fighting back against its imprisonment in a rigid stereotype that sees them only as a taciturn, hard-working "model minority" incapable of relating to others. At the forefront of the struggle is a new generation of writers, whose literary creations are finally reflecting a more multifaceted image of the people whose families came from many different countries with hugely diverse traditions and histories.

VANESSA HUA
Photographs by Josh Edelson

A street in San Francisco's
Chinatown.

When I first encountered High Expectations Asian Dad, I laughed out loud. The internet meme features a photo of a dour older Korean man haranguing his children about studying, demanding perfect scores, grades, and musical achievements.

Variously, he asks, "99% in exam? I have no son."

"What is difference between A- and A+? My love for you."

"You're five years old? When I was your age, I was six."

There's even a South Asian version of the meme that refers to Kamala Harris, the half-Indian, half-Black vice-president of the United States who was born and raised outside of San Francisco: "Why only 'vice-president'? Why not actual president?" the father asks.

It parodies Asian-American parents as people whose goal in life is to turn their children into academic superstars, violin and piano prodigies—an extreme version of the American Dream, which promises that if you work hard you will succeed in what's billed as the land of equal opportunity.

My own Chinese-immigrant parents dreamed big for me, their American-born daughter whom they raised in the suburbs east of San Francisco. After my older cousin scored perfectly on his SAT, the high-stakes college-entrance exam, we learned that sixteen students in the United States had also answered every question correctly that year. My father's response? "Getting a perfect score isn't as hard as I thought it would be."

Sure, Dad.

I had no doubt of his love, though. He taught me how to cross-country ski on Lake Tahoe's pristine trails in eastern California and also how to drive a car. To help me practice sharp turns, my father built a training module out of PVC pipes that I drove through again and again in an empty parking lot. And he was far more complex than any model minority depicted in the popular imagination. He loved to cruise San Francisco Bay on his red sailboat and to belt along to movie musicals, with their soaring songs, hero's journeys, and reversals of fortune, their extravagant declarations of bravery and love that captured the promise and perils of coming here.

VANESSA HUA is a columnist for the *San Francisco Chronicle* and the author of *A River of Stars*, *Deceit and Other Possibilities* and *Forbidden City*. A National Endowment for the Arts Literature Fellow, she has also received a Rona Jaffe Foundation Writers' Award, the Asian/Pacific American Award for Literature and a Steinbeck Fellowship in Creative Writing. She has filed stories from China, Burma, South Korea, Panama and Ecuador, and her work has appeared in publications including *The New York Times*, *The Washington Post* and *The Atlantic*. The daughter of Chinese immigrants, she lives in the San Francisco Bay Area with her family.

Like many Asian immigrants of his generation, he might have welcomed being labeled as hard-working and successful, but I'll never know for certain. A few years ago, he passed away before we had a chance to talk about what it means to be considered a model minority.

I wish we could have discussed the origins and consequences of this myth. He would have been proud of how Asian-American novelists from California are resisting and remaking the dominant narrative—one born out of the Cold War. If the United States was to win the global propaganda battle with the Soviet Union, it had to prove that democracy was superior and that poor countries should follow their lead. In a democracy, in a meritocracy, discrimination and racism weren't supposed to exist. Yet the civil rights movement of the 1950s and 1960s contradicted all that, as African Americans fought to gain equal rights in the United States.

The backlash against this struggle took many forms. In January 1966, sociologist William Petersen wrote a magazine article for *The New York Times* entitled, "Success Story: Japanese American Style." Later that year, *U.S. News & World Report* published "Success Story for One Minority Group in the United States." Both articles claimed Asian Americans overcame discrimination to achieve success; more pieces followed, crediting the community's triumphs to traditional family structure, Confucian values—respect for parents, loyalty to government, and keeping to one's place in society—and the work ethic. To quote *U.S. News*: "At a time when Americans are awash in worry over the plight of racial minorities, one such minority, the nation's 300,000 Chinese Americans, is winning wealth and respect by dint of its own hard work ... Still being taught in Chinatown is the old idea that people

DOUGHNUT KINGS

If the doughnut is the quintessential American sweet treat, Los Angeles is its capital, with over 1,500 doughnut shops. And doughnuts have always been a symbol of integration: they have an across-the-board appeal and are loved by every section of society, they are relatively easy to make and, at least in their simplest form, can be found in almost every culinary tradition around the world. Above all, doughnut shops were, and still are, very often run by immigrants, originally Asian, nowadays Latin American. The boom began in the late 1970s, when Cambodian refugee Ted Ngoy bought his first Christy's Donuts. In the space of ten years, during which he lived in a motorhome to move quickly between his branches and buy new ones, Ngoy was able to consolidate his successful chain and gain a reputation as the "Donut King" (also the title of his autobiography, self-published in 2018). His main competitor was another Asian American, of Japanese origin, Frank Watase, who made a big success of his Yum Yum chain and later Winchell's, which he bought in 2004, making him the main player on the Los Angeles scene. It is harder these days to hit the sweet spot in the world of the doughnut, however, and more recent waves of immigrants, mainly from South America, find it a less attractive prospect: while the Asians of the 1970s often came from trading backgrounds, the Latinos are mostly arriving from rural areas and have less experience in running companies.

Percentage of immigrants in the population of California and the USA, 1860–2019

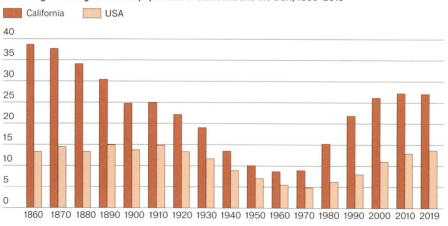

Change in the ethnic makeup of California, 1970–2020

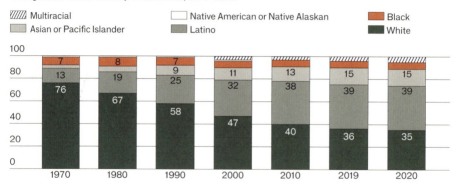

Origins of recent immigrants to California

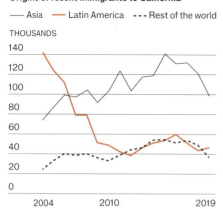

Legal status of immigrants in California

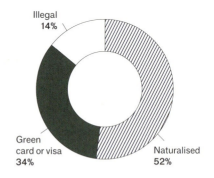

SOURCE: PUBLIC POLICY INSTITUTE OF CALIFORNIA

> "For Asian Americans, we might reverse the question and ask, 'How does it feel to be a solution?' That is to say, to have their bodies, their children, and their people exemplified?"

should depend on their own efforts—not a welfare check—in order to reach America's 'Promised Land.'"

The subtext of such articles—"If Asian Americans are 'making it' in this country, why can't Blacks?"—is a false equivalency, claiming that the discrimination Asian Americans faced was identical to that of slavery, segregation, and police brutality.

In *The Souls of Black Folk*—a pioneering work of sociology and African-American literature first published in 1903—W.E.B. Du Bois famously asks, "How does it feel to be a problem?" That is to say, African Americans have their bodies, their children, and their people maligned—their very existence a difficulty that needs solving.

For Asian Americans, we might reverse the question and ask, "How does it feel to be a solution?" That is to say, to have their bodies, their children, and their people exemplified? This sudden embrace and elevation of Asian Americans as model minorities is suspicious, given America's long history of xenophobia against them.

In 1849, the discovery of gold in California drew fortune seekers from around the world, and many Chinese people escaped economic chaos in their homeland. In the years that followed, politicians, unions, and businesses condemned the Chinese for taking away jobs and driving down wages of American workers. By 1882, Congress passed the Chinese Exclusion Act, which barred Chinese laborers from coming to this country. For the first time, the US stopped being a nation that welcomed

foreigners without restrictions and began to exert controls at the border and within the country—based on race, class, and gender. The first immigration law in the United States was designed to keep out Chinese. They were viewed as un-American, perpetual foreigners whose loyalties lay elsewhere, who didn't belong among whites or Blacks. There were limited loopholes, allowing merchants and scholars and a few others to come in, but immigration from China plummeted for decades. More laws followed against migrants from other parts of Asia.

Congress repealed the Exclusion Act in 1943 when China became an ally of the United States during the Second World War. Yet policies, on the whole, all but banned most immigration from Asia. It wasn't until 1965 that new laws were passed designed to attract skilled professionals, scientists, and engineers to the United States.

My parents arrived shortly before that wave after being awarded graduate-school fellowships in the Midwest. My mother would go on to earn a doctorate in biochemistry and my father in engineering. They met, married, and made their way to California.

The Golden State is now home to the largest Asian-American population in the country, with more than six million residents—about 17 per cent of the state's population overall and the fastest-growing ethnic group in the United States. Of the twenty-two million Asian Americans in the United States, a little under a third live in California.

Above top: People walk along a closed section of road in San Francisco's Chinatown. Chinatowns across America were hit particularly hard as the Covid-19 pandemic ravaged businesses nationwide.
Above bottom: Asians With Attitudes member Sakhone Lasaphangthong takes a photo of a pro-Asian mural while on patrol in Oakland's Chinatown district.

Despite the growing numbers, those in power continue to use the perceived socioeconomic success of Asian Americans as a racial wedge against other minorities and to downplay the impact of structural racism on Blacks and Latinos. Over the decades, this dynamic has played out again and again. Consider the debates over affirmative action and race-conscious admissions to elite high schools and colleges that pit Asian Americans against other minority groups.

Jennifer Lee, a professor of sociology at Columbia University, explained in an interview with CBC radio how Asian Americans are used to attack affirmative action—the controversial policy aimed at increasing educational opportunities for underrepresented groups. A 2018 lawsuit against Harvard University was orchestrated by a white conservative, who sought out Asian-American plaintiffs after he failed to win another case in which he'd backed a white woman who'd sued the University of Texas. As Lee put it, "This has little to do with Asian Americans. Asian Americans are being used as pawns … in his fight."

The battle over admissions continued more recently in California at Lowell, San Francisco's most prestigious public high school. In the past, enrollment did not reflect the demographics of the district overall: more than half the students identified as Asian American, 18 per cent white, 11.5 per cent Latino, and 2 per cent Black. As of the fall of 2021, Lowell no longer uses a combination of middle-school grades and state testing scores to admit most prospective students, instead using a lottery system that's in place elsewhere in the city. Board members who voted in favor of the change wanted to combat systemic racism and increase student diversity. Now, out of the 644

MATERNITY HOTELS

The law granting citizenship to anyone born on US soil was designed to regularise those who had been freed from slavery, and today it guarantees fundamental rights for the children of immigrants. As a consequence, a birth tourism sector has developed in the USA, the extent of which varies according to estimates (and the political spin of the person doing the calculation). In California, the most popular state, an industry has sprung up to serve these travellers, who mostly arrive from China; it is a practice at the limits of legality for the couples (although not actually illegal), and it will mean their offspring will have to make a difficult choice when they turn twenty-one because China does not allow dual citizenship. The parents undertake the trip to give their children the opportunities to study and work that a US passport would provide. It is a branch of tourism aimed at high-ranking individuals, requiring a significant investment in travel plus accommodation at one of the so-called "maternity hotels" catering to foreigners wishing to give birth on US soil. The police can do very little to stop it, apart from exploiting various customs issues. In California a task force has been set up to identify the hotels implicated, but very few have ever actually been shut down. In 2019 a 41-year-old hotel owner received a ten-month sentence after teaching her Chinese customers to lie about the reasons for their trip to the USA. This was not long enough for the prosecution, however, as they wanted an exemplary punishment to serve as a warning.

newly enrolled freshmen, nearly a quarter are Hispanic and 5 per cent are Black. Some parents have objected, calling the subsequent decline in Asian enrollment an example of anti-Asian racism. While I understand why they're worried and angry, their complaints are a far cry from what the originators of the term "Asian American" had intended. Coined at the University of California, Berkeley in 1968 in an act of self-determination, "Asian American" stood for a political agenda of equality, anti-racism, and anti-imperialism. Activists called for solidarity among Asians of all ethnicities, as well as Africans, Latinos, and Native Americans.

Yuri Kochiyama—the California-born Japanese-American activist at Malcom X's side when he was assassinated—offered this advice: "Don't become too narrow. Live fully ... Life is not what you alone make it. Life is the input of everyone who touched your life and every experience that entered it. We are all part of one another."

Today, demographers use "Asian American" as a label that encompasses people who trace their roots to more than twenty countries in East Asia, Southeast Asia, and the Indian subcontinent. The biggest groups include people of Chinese, Indian, and Filipino descent, followed by those with ancestry in Vietnam, Korea, and Japan—all with different cultures, languages, religions, geographies, class, education, and histories.

So what do Asian Americans have in common, then? *Racial Melancholia, Racial Dissociation: On the Social and Psychic Lives of Asian Americans* (Duke University Press, 2019)—a book that explores the social and psychic predicaments of young Asian Americans—argues what Asian Americans share is a long history of discrimination: "cast as an economic

TEHRANGELES

Between Sunset Boulevard, Beverly Hills and Santa Monica lies the neighbourhood of Westwood, although it is now known to Angelenos (and recently also Google Maps) as Tehrangeles or Little Persia. The area is home to over 500,000 Iranians, the largest community outside their native country, most of whom arrived after the Islamic Revolution of 1979. The diplomatic tensions between Washington and Tehran following the storming of the US embassy in the Iranian capital, when fifty-two officials were held hostage between 1979 and 1981, also impacted on the expatriate community, with incidences of racism and anti-Iranian demonstrations, so at the time, the residents of Tehrangeles preferred to pass themselves off as Italian or Greek or call themselves Persians in the hope of distancing themselves from the newly created Islamic theocracy – a very painful state of affairs, particularly for a community that saw Los Angeles as a temporary refuge, if anything, never as a permanent home. Forty years later the story has changed radically, partly thanks to a TV series entitled *Shahs of Sunset* (as in Sunset Boulevard), a reality show (made by the same producer as *Keeping Up With the Kardashians*) charting the lives of a group of very wealthy inhabitants of Tehrangeles, which ran for nine seasons with two reunions. The cast live in the lap of luxury, showing off their wealth and negotiating a world of shopping, love affairs and supercars. For some it painted an offensive and unfair picture through its superficial materialism; for others it was chiefly an entertaining bit of escapism that turned the spotlight on a community of immigrants and, in so doing, suggested an indirect form of acceptance.

threat and hyper-productive automatons and hence pathological to the U.S. nation-state ... refusal to see Asian Americans as a part and parcel of the American melting pot is less an individual failure to blend in ... than a legally and socially sanctioned interdiction."

The authors, David Eng—a professor of English and comparative literature— and Shinhee Han, a psychotherapist, describe the model-minority stereotype as "nerdy automatons" gifted in math and science, always working, compliant, wealthy, and free from discrimination. It's a pervasive stereotype. Time and again I've encountered Asian-American characters in novels, movies, and television shows who are cold and analytical, utterly lacking in people skills. Repeated and repeated, such tropes harden into the only truth afforded to Asian Americans. It's what novelist Chimamanda Ngozi Adichie described in her 2009 TED talk "The Danger of a Single Story": "The problem with stereotypes is not that they are untrue, but that they are incomplete," she said. "They make one story become the only story. It robs people of dignity. It makes our recognition of our equal humanity difficult. It emphasizes how we are different rather than how we are similar."

To be viewed as a "model" is to be viewed as not quite human, incapable of messy interiority and impulses. A new generation of literature, written by Asian-American authors from California, gives me hope. Their art resists the simplistic Black–white binary of race relations. Although America's history remains entangled in the legacy of slavery, narratives that ignore the experiences of people of Indigenous, Asian, Latino, and mixed descent fail to reflect the world we live in. Yet far too often critiques of late-stage capitalism don't address how people of color get pitted against each other.

Alexandra Chang's novel, *Days of Distraction* (Ecco, 2020), skillfully portrays the mental calculations, the considerations of race and power that her narrator makes in something so mundane as an editorial meeting at a tech magazine. When the managing editor uses the N-word, the narrator grapples with whether she should stay silent in the hopes that she might get the raise she's been asking for. She also realizes that the editorial staff has no Black men or women. "How had I not noticed? I worry that somebody else in the room is just noticing this at the same time as me, that they are looking at the few of us who are different in the same way we are looking at ourselves in that moment, as painfully not-them, as other. Or worse, I worry they are not noticing anything amiss at all," writes Chang, who grew up in Northern California.

In 2020, in the wake of George Floyd's death at the hands of police and after other cases of police brutality hit headlines, Asian Americans had to reckon with the anti-Blackness in themselves and in their communities. They are not white, but, like everyone in the United States, they are shaped by the systems of power that they were born into or discovered after they arrived. If they fail to speak up,

"A new generation of literature, written by Asian-American authors from California, gives me hope. Their art resists the simplistic Black–white binary of race relations."

A boy runs across the road near the Dim Sum Corner restaurant in San Francisco.

> "Some Asian Americans came as immigrants with savings, others as refugees or asylum seekers, driven from their homelands very often because of US involvement there."

if they fail to act, are they complicit? And how do they reckon with this prejudice in their own family?

Steph Cha, a Korean American born and raised in Southern California, homes in on this dilemma in her award-winning novel, *Your House Will Pay* (Ecco, 2019, USA / Faber and Faber, 2020, UK). The lives of two families collide. Back in the early 1990s—around the time police brutally beat motorist Rodney King—Grace Park's mother, a convenience store clerk, gunned down Ava Matthews, a Black teenager. Years later, Grace discovers this family secret and grapples with what her mother did. She asks why her sister Miriam can't forgive their mother. "I think if you love someone well enough, their evil makes you evil," Miriam tells her. "It doesn't matter that Ava Matthews was taller than Mom. She was a kid. Mom shot a kid in the back of the head. You don't want to think Mom's a bad person, but to think otherwise, you have to contort yourself to justify a murder—and if you bend too much that way, you'll become a different person. A worse person." Grace, who still lives with her parents, focuses on the sacrifice they made for her and her sister. Her sister Miriam has resisted that, but it's come at the cost of estrangement.

What I admire about the novel is how compelling the conversations can be when the characters not only consider individual striving but the systems of power and oppression into which they are embedded.

Statistically speaking, Asian Americans have higher educational levels, higher incomes, and lower rates of unemployment compared to other groups. But that's only in the aggregate. The blanket category masks the vast differences between Asian subgroups—education, socioeconomic levels, immigration status, disabilities visible and invisible, colonized or not—between and within ethnicities, within communities, or even within a single family for that matter. Some were born here. Some are undocumented—about eleven million in this country. Some came as immigrants with savings, others as refugees or asylum seekers, driven from their homelands very often because of US involvement there.

Take, for example, the war in Vietnam. Aimee Phan's *We Should Never Meet* (Picador, 2005) is a linked-short-story collection inspired by Operation Babylift, the evacuation of thousands of orphans from Vietnam to the United States weeks before the fall of Saigon. Phan—born and raised in Southern California—writes about Mai and Vinh, two orphans who grew up in the foster-care system in Orange County, a region home to one of the largest Vietnamese communities outside of Vietnam. They each have a different take on what it means to be a model minority. Mai enters an essay contest, writing about the hardships in her life, and wins scholarships for college. When the principal introduces her at a school assembly, he declares her "such a lucky girl with fortunate opportunities." Mai disagrees. "He probably meant to be

Above top: Jimmy Bounphengsy, a member of Asians With Attitudes, a movement that wants to unite all Asian Americans in the fight against racism, at the start of a patrol in Oakland's Chinatown.
Above bottom: Two young Asians hold fortune cookies asserting the Asian-American community's support of the Black Lives Matter protests.

complimentary, but the words bristled her ego. Lucky. Fortunate ... It wasn't luck. Yes, she was once the poor orphan child, but she had earned this. Since middle school, she had worked to ensure a future other children already inherited."

By contrast, Vinh's life has been more chaotic, and he ends up in a gang with his foster brothers, who prey on other Vietnamese. They know people in the community keep large sums of cash at home because they don't trust the banking system and are also afraid to go to the police for any reason. He's convinced that he's doing a favor to those he robs. "All of them in such a delusion about attaining this material dream of fortune and comfort, but at what expense? Didn't they realize they'd always be under the thumb of this government? It wasn't any better than Vietnam just because this government was more successful at deluding their people. They were fools to believe they could actually live among the Americans and become one of them. They never would. They would never be allowed." The inclusion of both narratives makes the telling of each more compelling. Having more than one character of that ethnic background opens up narrative possibilities. That multiplicity is not only more reflective of the world we live in but also makes for more interesting storytelling.

Nancy Jooyoun Kim—born and raised in Los Angeles—examines the intersection of race and class in her bestselling debut, *The Last Story of Mina Lee* (Park Row, 2020, USA / Headline Review, 2021, UK). At first, Mina, a newly arrived immigrant from South Korea, strikes up a friendship with Latino workers in Los Angeles. Her boss, Mr. Park, tells her that he worked very hard and now he's the owner. "You see what happens when you work hard? It pays off." Mina doesn't buy that explanation; everyone she knew worked hard but didn't own much of anything. Later, her boss notices she's become friends with the Mexican workers, but he warns, "They can't help that they don't, you know ... have the business sense. At least they work hard, you know?" She grows upset, silently questions him, but says nothing. Then he offers her a promotion, to the cash register, which she accepts. The job is better paid and less difficult physically. She sees how her Korean boss is trying to pit workers against each other, rejects it, but in the end still acquiesces to the system. She sees no other choice. Imagine if her character had bought into the boss's explanation for success, if she also subscribed wholly to the American Dream narrative?

Asian Americans are not a monolith, but so often they are portrayed as one. It's more than just an annoyance; such attitudes can lead to violence and hate crimes. During the pandemic, anti-Asian attacks skyrocketed in California and across the country. To shift the blame for America's woes, then-President Trump and his associates dubbed Covid-19 the "Wuhan virus," "Chinese virus," and "Kung Flu."

In *Time* magazine in 2020, Viet Thanh Nguyen—a Pulitzer Prize-winning novelist and MacArthur Foundation Genius Grant awardee—wrote about the roots of this hatred: "It is easier to blame a foreign country or a minority, or even politicians who negotiate trade agreements, than to identify the real power: corporations and economic elites who shift jobs, maximize profit at the expense of workers and care nothing for working Americans," writes Nguyen, a Vietnamese refugee who grew up in San Jose, the largest city

"During the pandemic, anti-Asian attacks skyrocketed. To shift the blame for America's woes, then-President Trump and his associates dubbed Covid-19 the 'Wuhan virus,' 'Chinese virus,' and 'Kung Flu.'"

in Northern California. "To acknowledge this reality is far too disturbing for many Americans, who resort to blaming Asians as a simpler answer."

And yet, some Asian Americans still can't help but hope that they might be the exception and that American exceptionalism is enough. Charles Yu—a Taiwanese American who grew up in Los Angeles—wrote a darkly funny critique of these tropes, the ways in which they limit Asian Americans, and the illusion of social mobility in America. *Interior Chinatown* (Pantheon, 2020, USA / Europa Editions, 2021, UK) winner of the 2020 National Book Award, is told in the form of a screenplay. The protagonist, Willis Wu, lists on his résumé the stereotypical roles he's played as they appear in the screen credits: Disgraced Son, Delivery Guy, Silent Henchman, Caught Between Two Worlds, Guy Who Runs in and Gets Kicked in the Face, Striving Immigrant, and Generic Asian Man. As a bit player on the procedural cop show *Black and White*, he's hoping someday to become Kung Fu Guy—the most respected role that anyone who looks like him can attain. The two leads are the White Lady Cop and the Black Dude Cop. It's a different story, though, for actors of Asian descent. "There's just something about Asians that makes reality a little too real, overcomplicates the clarity, the duality, the clean elegance of Black and White, the proven template ... You wonder: can you change it? Can you be the one that actually

breaks through?" Even as Wu gets bigger and bigger roles, it's a game he can't win. It's rigged, always just out of reach. Even when Asian Americans attain the outward trappings of success, they may become a target. They become exposed, their qualifications used against them, past and present (see "Hollywood on Hollywood" on page 182).

The novels I've mentioned are just a few recent ones by California authors who subvert old, harmful narratives. Ultimately, such fiction fosters empathy. You may have heard about the experiment in which people performed better on tests measuring empathy, social perception, and emotional intelligence after reading literary fiction. Those skills are necessary to gauge what someone else might be thinking or feeling, skills that are much needed in the age of chaos and division.

In my own work over the years, whether in journalism or in fiction, set here or abroad, I've tried to shine a light on untold stories, ones that might inspire a change in thinking and a change in action and subvert the model minority myth.

High Expectations Dad would expect nothing less. My father, too.

I can't wait to share these Asian-American novels with my ten-year-old twin sons. Fiction has the power to deepen the collective understanding of our very different lives and pave the way for an even greater abundance in the future. 🖋

Shadows in the Valley

Francisco Cantú

For millions of Americans as well as tourists, Yosemite National Park represents an ideal of unsullied nature, perpetuated through family stories and the nation's epic narratives. But if we ignore the history of violence and genocide behind the park's creation, we risk doing wrong not only to the victims but also to ourselves, because in taking this approach we are denied the chance to fully understand – and therefore to truly love – a place as intrinsically linked to its human past and present as it is to its rocks and its waterfalls.

Photographs by George Rose

W e arrived in Yosemite as summer turned to autumn, just as cold began to bite the evening air and the first green leaves of maple flashed yellow. Despite having visited on several previous occasions, this iconic park—the crown jewel of California—was still a place that felt unknown and overwhelming to me. But for my partner, it was a place that had, for more than half a century, served as a site of yearly family communion, a place where her grandparents' ashes were scattered across the high meadows and where her aging father and uncles continued to return as often as they could with their own children, revisiting old trails and campsites and recounting the glory days when they had spent long summer weeks roaming the park as a pack of feral boys. On this trip, however, my partner and I were traveling alone. It had, in fact, been months since we had seen our loved ones in the flesh, months since we had even left the confines of our home, our neighborhood, our city.

Before leaving Arizona, we had waited anxiously for negative test results to confirm that we were not silent carriers of the virus, monitoring all the while the fires growing across central California, choking the state with smoke. To reach Yosemite, we had driven for thirteen hours, leaving early in the morning and arriving long after dark. Along the way, we avoided stepping indoors at all costs, donning masks whenever we left the car and sanitizing our hands each time we filled our tank with ever more expensive gas. Our final destination was a Park Service cabin in the heart of Yosemite Valley, where two of our best friends,

FRANCISCO CANTÚ is a writer, translator and the author of *The Line Becomes a River* (Riverhead, 2018, USA / Vintage, 2019, UK), winner of the 2018 Los Angeles Times Book Prize and a finalist for the National Book Critics Circle Award in non-fiction. A former Fulbright fellow, he has been the recipient of a Pushcart Prize, a Whiting Award and an Art for Justice fellowship. His writing and translations have been featured in *The New Yorker*, *Best American Essays*, *Harper's* and *Guernica* as well as on the radio show *This American Life*. A lifelong resident of the Southwest, he now lives in Tucson, where he coordinates the Field Studies in Writing Program at the University of Arizona.

GEORGE ROSE's photographic career has spanned almost fifty years, during which time he has been named California Newspaper Photographer of the Year (1976), won a World Press Photo award (1987) and been nominated twice for a Pulitzer Prize. His work has focused primarily on the entertainment industry and popular culture as well as news, politics and sport and has been featured in *USA Today*, *Time*, *Newsweek* and *Rolling Stone*.

who work for the park, were living for the season. By the time we arrived, April and Dustin were already preparing for bed and greeted us at the door in their pajamas. After sharing a strangely tentative embrace, they helped us unload our things, and we realized this was the first time we had stepped foot in someone else's home or touched another human being in more than half a year.

The next morning, I awoke early and joined April in the kitchen. She was already dressed in her park ranger's uniform, and, for a moment, as I struggled to fight away the fog of sleep, I experienced a brief childhood vision of my mother dressed in the very same gray shirt and green pants, her black hair spilling out from an identical flat-brimmed hat. I snapped out of my stupor when April asked if I had seen the view outside. I shook my head, and she led me to the front porch, opening the door and gesturing up toward the towering reaches of Yosemite Falls, its postcard image visible through a mist-like veil of smoke. April began to explain how each year in the springtime waterways in the park would rush with snowmelt. The pounding of the falls, she said, becomes so loud that she often finds it hard to sleep. But now, at the end of another severe dry season, only a black stain could be seen on the cliffs. Lately, April said, she and Dustin used this view of the dry falls primarily as a way to gauge the smoke. Today it seemed moderate, but thick enough that she still advised me to wear a mask out of doors.

In the coming days, the smoke in the park became worse, and instead of hiking and exploring the myriad trails and backcountry landmarks, my partner and I stayed shuttered indoors with our friends, huddled around their endlessly humming air purifier. The Yosemite Valley, usually crowded with cars and wandering tourists, was already quieter than usual, since the park was operating at 50 per cent capacity in response to the shutdowns gripping the state, the country, the globe. But as smoke thickened in the Sierra, the valley became emptier from one day to the next and soon began to take on a lonesome and ghostly air, with its emblematic domes, stone peaks, and monolithic rock faces lurking behind a grim haze.

As the surrounding fires continued to grow, the park finally closed to the public altogether. Marooned in our friends' cabin, we escaped briefly each evening to walk through the abandoned meadows with our masks on, soaking in the eerie silence. As the single busiest place in the entire park, the Yosemite Valley is easily the most heavily trafficked outdoor attraction in all of California, and we knew that these few days of closure offered a rare respite of calm. It was almost as if the wildlife sensed this, too, understanding that they had been given a rare chance to reassert their dominion over the place. We observed groups of California mule deer wandering the usually clogged roadways and saw black bear mothers leading their cubs along paved bike paths. We even watched as one adolescent bear swayed precariously above an intersection in the high branches of a massive oak, foraging the season's final explosion of acorns.

Walking through the valley, I reveled in the assumption that I was seeing it at its emptiest, and I even began to imagine that I was looking through a widening window into the planet's unpeopled future. I soon confessed to our friends that I was finding a strange pleasure in these seemingly apocalyptic scenes—a feeling rooted, I realized, in the same selfishness that many of us feel in America's national parks, or in any place perceived as wild, a sensation rooted in the urge to possess, briefly, a piece of nature's majesty for ourselves, to feel that we are alone in our communion with the sublime. The usually bustling atmosphere of the valley had long caused me to write it off as a place

impossible to experience solitude, almost causing me to dismiss it altogether. When I confessed this to Dustin, who works as a wildlife biologist for the park, he remained strangely silent. His work has led him to visit many of Yosemite's most remote corners, and when I asked him what his favorite place in the park was, expecting him to describe some glorious and seldom-seen vista, he told me, to my great surprise, that his favorite place was right here in the valley. When I asked why, he answered simply: *it feels like people belong here.*

Long before American settlers began to refigure Yosemite as one of the country's foremost sites to experience a primeval fantasy of wilderness, it served as a central gathering place for the area's Indigenous inhabitants and was, for millennia, shaped by their presence. My idea of walking through the valley without seeing another person, I realized, flowed from the mythology of America's national parks, from grand narratives I had heard since childhood positioning nature and landscape as a kind of monument. As I began to recognize the extent to which this mythology reached deep into my consciousness, I also wondered what it meant that so many Americans tie parts of their identity to this place, returning here again and again, generation after generation. What story, I began to wonder, do families pass on about themselves here, what impressions do they hold about their place in the landscape of California, the West, and America writ large? And if Yosemite is, indeed, a place of communion, what is it that gets consecrated here—the old colonial urge to imagine oneself as a lone figure in the wild, or the sheer magnetic force of the stone walls and shifting waters that have for so long drawn humans to gather together and gaze out across the land?

*

My mother and I were both born in California but spent little time there, almost as if the state were too densely populated to accommodate our predilection for feeling close to the sprawl of nature. The early years of my childhood played out inside a national park profoundly different from Yosemite. The Guadalupe Mountains, where my mother worked as an interpretive park ranger, is one of the least visited parks in the United States, located in a remote corner of the West Texas desert. It is a place that, despite its vastness, always seemed far more comprehensible to me than the abundant forests and waterways of California. In the desert, the small cast of plant and animal life was far easier to make sense of—even its peaks and ranges seemed more digestible, "sky islands" rising up from the arid sea around them rather than the endless mountains beyond mountains of the Sierra Nevada.

But the main reason the desert always felt so much more intelligible, I realize now, is because of the stories I grew up with, stories that served to make sense of the landscape and its creatures. As an interpretive ranger, my mother's duties were not just to help protect and preserve the natural beauty of parklands but, more specifically, to interpret the stories of those places for visitors by describing the interconnectedness of the flora, the fauna, and the human inhabitants that mingled there throughout history. Storytelling wasn't just something my mother did for work—she told stories at home, too, at a time when my mind was just beginning to grasp and file away memories. Living in the Guadalupes, we had to drive over an hour and a half to reach the nearest grocery store, and on our weekly trips to the city the highway across the desert was so empty that we often saw more jackrabbits than passing cars. I loved my mother's stories so much back then that during these long drives I would beg her to tell me tales to pass the time, one after another. These requests would often exhaust her, and it wasn't long before she implemented a new rule, refusing to tell me another story until I told her one in return. As a four-year-old, I would insist that I didn't know any stories, but my mother simply pointed toward the horizon, asking me to describe what I saw. I quickly learned to name the passing features. I see peaks and clouds, I told her. Rocks and sand. Birds and rabbits. Well, my mother would say, make a story about them.

Soon, storytelling became an easy exchange between my mother and I, one I came to understand as profoundly rooted in one's surroundings. This is also how, ever since I can remember, I was made to look to the landscape for inspiration and guidance—a place where I could connect with a deeper sense of self. In those early days, I came to perceive the windswept mountains and Permian canyons of the Guadalupes as altogether free of confusion or darkness, and I found it impossible to imagine, even for a moment, that such places might be made to hold anything other than beauty.

As an adult, I have slowly begun to realize how, for my mother, stories about place and landscape largely superseded the family stories that so often first shape the ways we see ourselves and our place in the world. Throughout the entirety of my childhood, for example, I cannot remember ever discussing with her the fact that my grandfather was an immigrant, that his consciousness had been forged in another language, another country. I don't remember anyone ever telling me that he was Mexican or that I, in some small but meaningful way, was too. I now realize that my mother barely understood this herself. Growing up, she possessed a single photograph of her father and retained only the haziest memory of him holding her as an infant. Her parents' early separation meant that she was raised by a single mother far away from him, not knowing the sound of his voice, the touch of his hands, or the stories or places that shaped him.

Perhaps it was partially due to this absence of a father figure from her interior life that my mother often turned outward to construct an idea of herself, looking, most often, to the outdoor spaces that surrounded her to find meaning. After leaving California as a small child, my mother found her home in the Arizona desert, replete with its bewildering topography of deep canyons and rolling bajadas, hidden waters and dry washes, volcanic mesas and vast plateaus. This terrain was also one steeped in myth, a superimposed lore of discovery and solace that, for my mother, would have been far more accessible than her own family story. In this way, the landscape must have offered her an element of certainty, or, at least, the kind of mystery that could be understood and investigated, interpreted and described.

The stories my mother passed on to me did not deal with the exploits or misadventures of relatives and ancestors. Like her, I grew up without brothers and sisters, without aunts and uncles, without a cloud of cousins swirling around me, trafficking in family gossip. Instead, my mother passed on to me songs and folktales, stories of talking animals and forces of nature sprung to life. This, in turn, shaped how I came to understand myself and the world around me—not by discerning family lineage and lore but by learning the names of trees and rivers, the cycles of seasons and storms, the sounds and signs of creatures moving just outside our doors, always close and lingering around us.

After she became an interpretive ranger, my mother, a storyteller by nature, also became a storyteller by trade. As she moved from one park to another, her day-to-day job was to make comprehensible to visitors the history and ecology of some of the country's most recognizable scenery—the Great Smoky Mountains, Yellowstone, the Grand Canyon, Muir Woods—crafting narratives that would help anchor the visitors' sense of awe in science and cultural record. In a sense, this also meant that my mother was conscripted into the work of national myth-making, sometimes recounting state-crafted narratives time and again that, for all their romantic evocation, simplified and obscured the bloodshed long ago written into the American landscape. The wilderness that my mother and I held dear, the places that fed our soul and gave us meaning, were not only sites of preservation, I would learn, but of erasure as well. For my mother,

as for so many others, the stories of these cherished places, what the author and conservationist Terry Tempest Williams calls "the closest thing we have to sacred land," helped anchor her in the idea that wild spaces could fill a lacuna within. But even this dignified regard for the land is one that comes at great cost, a notion that flows, in spite of all its reverence, in an unbroken line from acts of violence that remain unabandoned and ongoing.

*

The name "Yosemite" can be traced back to a contingent of Indian-killers that marauded through California's High Sierra more than a century and a half ago. These men were, by most accounts, the first group of white people to lay eyes on what are now some of the most photographed sites on earth—Half Dome, El Capitan, Bridalveil Fall, Tuolumne Meadows. This company, known as the Mariposa Battalion, was formed with the express purpose of making war upon the Indigenous population and received enough financial backing from the legislature of the newly incorporated state of California to cause many of the recruits to regard the work of killing as more promising than that of mining, even amid the ongoing fever of the Gold Rush. One of the men who commanded this battalion, J. Neely Johnson, would later go on to become the state's governor, and at the time he plainly stated his desire to pursue the kind of warfare which, he wrote, "*must of necessity be one of extermination.*" Indeed, as described in the book *An American Genocide* by Benjamin Madley (Yale University Press, 2016), when the Mariposa Battalion entered the valleys, meadows, and mountain passes of Yosemite in 1851, they moved through them with fearsome efficiency, "systematically torching villages and food stores" and making survival difficult even for those attempting to retreat from the smoke-clogged killing fields.

Accompanying this battalion was a surgeon by the name of Lafayette Houghton Bunnell. Educated in New York, he was one of the few literate party members, and it is he who kept record of their travels and made the region known by its current name. "It would be better to give it an Indian name," asserted Bunnell, "than to import a strange and inexpressive one." After returning home from the massacre, he weighed in on the question of what to call the place, writing: "the name of the tribe who had occupied it would be more appropriate than any I had heard suggested. I then proposed that we give the valley the name of Yo-sem-i-ty, as it was suggestive, euphonious, and certainly American; that by so doing, the name of the tribe of Indians which we had met leaving their homes in this valley, perhaps never to return, would be perpetuated."

There are several sinister things about Bunnell's seemingly innocuous, well-intentioned quote. First and foremost, there is the use of the past tense: "the tribe who *had* occupied it ... perhaps never to return," as if he understood this as some natural fact rather than a forced expulsion underpinned by the idea of annihilation. And, second, there is his easy suggestion that "Yosemite" is an altogether "American" sounding name, pleasing to the ear despite its nonchalant appropriation of a culture wiped from their homes. "Yosemite," it turns out, wasn't what the people Bunnell encountered actually called themselves but rather a name used to describe them by a neighboring band of people, meaning something along the lines of "bear-killers" or "some of them are killers."

Despite the misinterpreted roots of the name, the fact is that in 1851, a state-sponsored band of two hundred white mercenaries successfully cleared out thousands of peaceful inhabitants from land now cherished the world over. The people who had lived in relationship with these valleys for more than eight thousand years were multitudinous—Ahwahnee, Miwok, Mono, Paiute, Chukchansi, among others. Whether through being killed in battle or dying from subsequent disease, malnourishment, and the trauma of being removed to faraway reservations, by the

THE PASSENGER   Francisco Cantú

time President Abraham Lincoln signed the Yosemite Land Grant thirteen years later, there were scarcely one hundred Indigenous people remaining within the new borders of the park.

The idea of national parks in America was, from the very beginning, formed in relationship to bloodshed. When Lincoln signed the Yosemite Land Grant in 1864, the country was still deep in the throes of the Civil War, which still officially stands as the bloodiest conflict ever waged in America's history. The new legislation protecting Yosemite was unprecedented, setting aside for the very first time a federally recognized nature reserve to be held in perpetuity for "preservation and public enjoyment." Photographs of Yosemite's stunning landmarks had already begun to proliferate across America, and the images represented a grandeur that Lincoln and others hoped would offer the kind of peace and solace that might serve to unify a nation and mend a bloodied national psyche.

After the establishment of the reserve, America's most celebrated landscape architect and the co-designer of New York's Central Park, Frederick Law Olmsted, was named as one of its first overseers. Olmsted soon became one of the foremost advocates for a nationwide system of parks and helped to define the philosophical underpinnings for administering public lands across the country. Setting aside and preserving wild spaces, he thought, could provide an antidote to the profound violence that had riven the nation, offering a place to calm one's spirit. "What we want to gain," Olmsted wrote, "is tranquility and rest to the mind."

Olmsted's thinking about public lands continued to define American discourse and policy on these matters well into the next century. Nearly fifty years later, Wallace Stegner, America's "Dean of Western Writers," argued that America's national parks had come to form "a geography of hope." Despite the genocide and removal that underlies so much federal land ownership, the notion of hope is still central to the predominant cultural discourse about the American outdoors. National parks have long been presented to us as someplace akin to church—places for reflection and clarity, untarnished sites of worship. But as history stalks our founding myths, the "hope" we might find in such places becomes something ever more dubious and ill defined.

*

Immigrant identity is frequently understood as something shaped by cycles of loss and reclamation, determined, most often, by outside forces—the violence of governments and poverty, the upheaval of societal rupture and cultural change. But when stories and traditions are left behind, new myths soon rise up to take their place, presaging the internal struggle that often lies ahead. Nowhere is this clearer than in California, a state that is home to more immigrants than any other in America. Here, the newcomer, their children, their children's children, are each progressively subsumed into the unwavering machinations of assimilation, venturing closer and closer to an identity that is almost always represented, subtly or not, as more desirable than their own.

There is, undoubtedly, a seldom-explored connection between the mythology of immigrant assimilation and the stories we tell about the American landscape. When the tangled roots that underlie our histories are obscured or denied, a void is inevitably introduced into our story—be it the story of family, the places they hold dear, or the nation they call home—a void that festers the longer it is ignored, that is passed on from one generation to the next until it is finally spoken aloud. This is the void my mother grappled with, the void I inherited from her. It is one, I have learned, that cannot be filled by communing with places presented as sacrosanct and hallowed, at least not as long as their histories remain unacknowledged and unreckoned with.

My family's most often recounted pieces of ancestral lore

seem to have always been rendered, like the mythology of the American wilderness, only in the broadest of strokes. I have long heard, for example, that as a child my grandfather and his siblings fled their home by taking a train in the dead of night through a countryside ravaged by the Mexican Revolution. As they neared the US border, the sun rose, and they watched in the dawn light as silhouettes emerged of bodies hanging from trees. But once they arrived in California as refugees, the story they most repeated was one that placed them beside long-dead kings and conquerors. The Cantús, various family members insisted, were descended from Spanish royalty and could trace our line directly to King Ferdinand and Queen Isabella, the monarchs who oversaw the final bloody act of the Reconquista and sponsored the first voyage of Columbus, two events that have torn at the fabric of history ever since. My grandfather and his siblings clung to this story—this supposed lineage buried more than four centuries behind them, on a continent they had never known, far more than they ever seemed to embrace their identity as Mexican, as if being tied to that place somehow threatened them with an otherness that was to be rejected swiftly and out of hand.

After settling in San Diego, my immigrant ancestors, with the benefit of their light skin, were quickly subsumed by new American lives. I suspect they learned to cling most forcefully to the fantasy placing them beside long-dead kings and conquerors during these early, formative years in the United States, when the value of claiming whiteness would have become even more apparent than in their homeland. In America, they would have quickly understood that *Mexican* meant *brown*, while *Spanish* carried a possible association with a continent always imagined to be superior. In this way, they also learned to erase themselves—or, more precisely, to erase the place they came from, expunging Mexico from their outward selves in ways both simple and profound. Such acts of reinvention are also a kind of disappearance—the slow and quiet replacement of one story with another, more powerful one. These inescapable narratives, which continue to estrange so many of us from ourselves, are fearsome not just for how they become ingrained into a national psyche but for the way they become so deeply woven into our own confused hearts, embedding themselves into the people and places that surround us, taking up residence even in the physical terrain, in the very soil we walk on.

The German writer W.G. Sebald was obsessed, in his life and in his art, with considering how the violence of the Second World War and the horrors of the Holocaust permeated the post-war culture of his home country and hovered within the memory of the entire continent of Europe. In one interview, he describes the region where he was born as "an idyllic place," one peppered with quaint villages graced with stunning views of the surrounding peaks and valleys. Sebald was born in 1944, almost exactly one year before Germany's surrender to the Allies, and in his book *On the Natural History of Destruction* (Modern Library, 2004, USA / Penguin, 2004, UK), he considers these earliest years of his life, writing: "I spent my childhood and youth on the northern outskirts of the Alps, in a region that was largely spared the immediate effects of the so-called hostilities. At the end of the war, I was just one year old, so I can hardly have any impressions of that period of destruction based on personal experience. Yet to this day, when I see photographs or documentary films dating from the war I feel as if I were its child, so to speak, as if those horrors I did not experience cast a shadow over me, and one from which I shall never entirely emerge."

This quote from Sebald is made in respect to historical events regarded almost universally as cataclysmic, as defining tragedies of the 20th century and of modern history. But perhaps this is what's missing from our understanding of the less recognized atrocities that have taken place on American soil—for so long our dominant culture has willfully failed to recognize these acts as tragedies that define us, dismissing them as road bumps

that need not weigh upon our conception of history. But as we shy away from reckoning with what has happened in the places we hold dear, we perpetuate an impoverished understanding of what it means to love a place. There is, in reality, no scenic grandeur magnificent enough to supersede the profundity of human loss, to prevent the violence of history from being embedded into a site's topographical memory. The only true way to honor a place we love, then, is to tell the fullness of its story, just as the only way to honor ourselves and our loved ones is to acknowledge the fullness of where we come from. For the millions of people who return to Yosemite year after year, tying generational memories to the peaks, lakes, and walls formed by vanished glaciers, a better understanding of the place also portends a better understanding of ourselves.

My last living immigrant ancestor, my great-aunt Frances, lived to the age of 102. More than a decade after her death, my cousins finally decided to sell her house in San Diego, a home that had provided shelter to our family for generations. A few months before it was placed on the market, my mother and I went to visit our cousins and sleep one last time beneath portraits of our forebears. During these final days, I awoke early to catalogue the contents of a massive chest more than a century old, filled with family documents and photographs, keepsakes and correspondence. The vast majority of the material was handwritten in Spanish with looping script on crumbling paper, words penned by great-grandparents who died long before my birth, by great-aunts and great-uncles I never knew. Inside, I discovered birth certificates and deeds, postcards and telegrams, receipts and business contracts, bills of sale and notices of debt, and pictures of unknown landscapes in Mexico, seemingly taken at the far edge of the Chihuahuan Desert, with blurred figures and thatched buildings lost in the middle distance.

The old chest also contained several boxes of photos from my family's early years in California—images of my great-grandfather working at the newsstand where he sold imported Mexican magazines and Spanish-language newspapers, pictures of my grandfather at work as a delivery boy, pictures of his sisters posing in flapper dresses and his brothers suited up for local dances in tuxedos and bow ties, and, later, pictures of them in uniform as soldiers being trained for war. There were also images from family trips up and down the length of California, pictures of my grandfather standing beside windswept beaches and giant redwoods. There, too, were photos of him as a young man posing triumphantly in the Yosemite Valley, standing tall with his hands on his hips and a look of self-assuredness on his face as unmistakable as the waterfalls and granite domes behind him. Yosemite was clearly a place where any insecurities he may have harbored about himself, about his place in this adopted country, had dissolved completely. It is a place, I am sure, where he must have found some sense of solace and belonging, a place where he would have felt grounded, comprehensible, and certainly American. 🐦

Super Trees

Although suffering devastating fires in recent years, California's reputation as a land of abundance is still legendary – a reputation epitomised by its huge and almost incomprehensibly ancient trees. Alongside the natural history they embody, they also have a human history attached to them. Over the years people have set out to measure these trees (by climbing them – no mean feat, with some sequoias standing over a hundred metres tall), they have named them (from mythology but very often with references to Tolkien), endeavoured to protect them (hiding their locations, wrapping them in fire blankets or buying the land on which they grow), studied them and attempted to exploit them.

General Grant

WHERE: Kings Canyon National Park
SCIENTIFIC NAME: *Sequoiadendron giganteum*
VOLUME: 1,320 m³

The world's second largest tree by volume. Over the years it has been honoured by several presidents: in April 1926 Calvin Coolidge proclaimed it the "Nation's Christmas Tree" (not to be confused with the "National Christmas Tree" in Washington, DC, which is decorated every Yuletide), while in 1956 Eisenhower dubbed it a national shrine dedicated to the country's war dead, the only living organism to join the list of national shrines in the USA.

Hyperion

WHERE: Redwood National Park
SCIENTIFIC NAME: *Sequoia sempervirens*
HEIGHT: 116 m

The world's tallest tree. As with all redwoods, the most accurate way of measuring the tree is to climb it: something of a challenge, given that the lowest branches strong enough to support an adult grow far beyond reach from the ground. At only six or seven hundred years old, Hyperion is relatively young as redwoods go. It was discovered by two scientists and measured by the pioneering researcher Stephen Sillett, who has climbed almost all of California's tallest conifers. Its exact location is kept secret to avoid acts of vandalism or visits by inconsiderate tourists.

General Sherman

WHERE: Sequoia National Park
SCIENTIFIC NAME:
Sequoiadendron
giganteum
VOLUME: 1,487 m³

Probably the largest
living organism on
earth by volume,
with a trunk
measuring eleven
metres in diameter.
In 2021, while
under threat
during the wildfire season, it
was wrapped in fire-retardant blankets
to protect it from damage and emerged
unscathed. It owes its name to a general
who fought on the Union side in the
American Civil War but was also known as
Karl Marx when the area where it grows
was home to a utopian community.

The Mother of the Forest

WHERE: Sierra Nevada, East Central
California
SCIENTIFIC NAME: *Sequoiadendron*
giganteum
LIFESPAN: 667 BCE–1856 CE

This huge specimen had its bark removed
to be put on display around the world, first in
New York, then in London, where it became
an exhibit at the Crystal Palace in the 1850s
under the name of the "Mammoth Tree"; it
was later destroyed in a fire. The tree itself
died shortly afterwards, before a spiral
staircase could be cut into it that would
have turned it into a panoramic viewing
point. The indiscriminate exploitation it
suffered led to outrage across the nation.

Bennett Juniper

WHERE: Stanislaus National Forest
SCIENTIFIC NAME: *Juniperus*
occidentalis
AGE: 3,000 years old (estimated)

Holding a double record as the world's
largest and also oldest juniper, it is the
focal point of a project run by the charity
Save the Redwoods, which protects
trees by buying the land on which they
grow and turning them into protected
areas. The tree, which has grown tough
in the face of the region's extreme
weather, was threatened by fires in
2018. It is also home to a marmot that
removes pieces of wood from the trunk
to make space for its burrow. According
to carbon-14 dating, some of these
pieces are two thousand years old.

Joshua tree

WHERE: Mojave Desert
SCIENTIFIC NAME: *Yucca brevifolia*
OCCUPATION: Rock star

Easily recognisable from their iconic silhouette, Joshua trees populate a landscape that conjures up images associated with Westerns and have often been used as cultural references – not least in lending their name to the multi-million-selling 1987 album by U2. It was given its moniker by Mormons crossing the desert who followed the directions indicated by its branches, which were raised up as if in supplication – or at least so legend would have it; there are no surviving contemporary documents to verify this story.

Methuselah

WHERE: Ancient Bristlecone Pine Forest
SCIENTIFIC NAME: *Pinus longaeva*
AGE: More than 4,850 years old

As the world's oldest living tree, its location is kept secret for security reasons. But it is not the only old-timer in the forest where it grows: other specimens nearby are also extremely ancient and, curiously, very different, to the extent that each of them can be seen as a unique, rugged individual, shaped in one way or another by millennia of snow and drought. Methuselah is said to be accompanied by a curse: best keep your distance if you don't want to risk an early demise.

Lone Cypress

WHERE: Pebble Beach
SCIENTIFIC NAME: *Hesperocyparis macrocarpa*
OCCUPATION: Influencer

Exposed roots clinging to the cliff edge, its crown lashed by the wind, the churning ocean below: Big Sur encapsulated in a single image – a seriously over-used image, given that the Lone Cypress is probably the most photographed tree in North America. Held secure by steel cables, it can be seen looking out over Carmel Bay from the nearby coastal toll road that passes through a resort and golfing destination, the Pebble Beach Golf Links. Since 1919 a representation of the tree has been the trademarked logo of the Pebble Beach Company, a legal status that the company says helps to protect the tree itself.

HOW THEY COMPARE

METRES

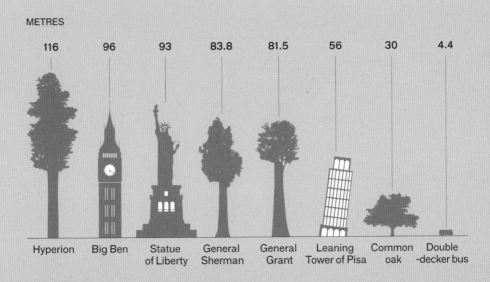

116	96	93	83.8	81.5	56	30	4.4
Hyperion	Big Ben	Statue of Liberty	General Sherman	General Grant	Leaning Tower of Pisa	Common oak	Double-decker bus

Tipping the World Over

From counterculture movements to the dominant culture, technological shifts to culinary trends, what happens in San Francisco and the Bay Area offers a sneak preview of what the rest of us will be doing a few years down the line. The Italian writer Michele Masneri, who was a news correspondent in California for a number of years, turns his European gaze on the space–time divide between Silicon Valley and the rest of the world, this time not as a correspondent from a foreign country but from the future.

MICHELE MASNERI
Translated by Oonagh Stransky
Photographs by Josh Edelson

A view of Alcatraz Island from San Francisco.

Frank Lloyd Wright once claimed that if you tipped the world over on its side, everything not firmly anchored to the ground would slide towards Los Angeles. It could also be said that if you tipped California over – Northern California in particular – everything would roll towards the rest of the world. There is probably no other place in the world that in recent times has given rise to so many changes that have gone on to affect the habits of so many people: app technology, social media, our obsession with natural foods and some sexual-health practices to name just a few. But how long might it take for such changes to roll down San Francisco's hills and reach my homeland, Italy? The first gourmet cafés only began appearing in Rome in 2021, but they were all the rage in San Francisco in 2016 and had already popped up in Berlin, Paris and London. The debate over cancel culture and feminism is now in full swing in Italy (again, about five years late). And, in the LGBTQ+ community, the PrEP pill, approved by the US Food and Drug Administration agency in 2012, is only now starting to gain traction in Europe.

It is this space–time schism that makes it interesting to look at Silicon Valley from a European perspective – specifically, in my case, that of an Italian. This is what I sought to do during my years as a correspondent in California between 2016 and 2018 and in subsequent trips there, and it is what I seek to do in this article. More than a correspondent from a foreign country, I wrote then and write now from the future, from space.

Northern California is a long way from Italy, not least in geographical terms. If you tell someone in Italy that you're based in Silicon Valley, they will say, "Oh, I thought you were in San Francisco." If you were to poll people, I think 90 per cent of respondents wouldn't know how to pinpoint the valley on a map. After all, California is by definition a remote place: it's the frontier, the Wild West, and Northern California even more so. For Europeans, the myths of Silicon Valley and of Northern California are as fascinating as they are nebulous. As a matter of fact, the name Silicon Valley is often used as a correlative, frequently in a fanciful way, as a contrast to a surrounding area ("the Silicon Valley of Sardinia" or "a Bavarian Silicon Valley"), making them sound like enchanted places, home to those magical creatures known as startuppers, people who inhabit mysterious caves (their garages), where they build companies that twenty years later eventually make their way to the Old World.

MICHELE MASNERI is a Rome-based journalist and author who writes about culture and society. He has worked with *Vogue Italia, Domus, AD, Wired US*. He is the design editor at *Il Foglio*, for which he was the Silicon Valley correspondent, and his reports from California were included in the collection *Steve Jobs non abita più qui* ("Steve Jobs No Longer Lives Here", Adelphi, 2020). His latest book is a biography of the Italian writer Alberto Arbasino, *Stile Alberto* (Quodlibet, 2021).

In 2003 nineteen-year-old Elizabeth Holmes founded the startup Theranos after leaving Stanford University. Her concept was a revolutionary device that would be easy to transport and able to carry out complex medical tests using a single drop of blood. She attracted large numbers of investors who believed the technology would change the face of healthcare, simplifying costly procedures and giving countless patients faster access to routine tests. In 2014 Theranos was valued at $9 billion, and Holmes, with her black polo-neck reminiscent of Steve Jobs, ended up on the cover of a number of prestigious magazines. Then an investigation by *The Wall Street Journal* revealed the truth about Holmes's promises: the equipment did not work, the data were unreliable and the figures had been massaged. Her reputation and the company's valuation collapsed. In early 2022 Holmes was convicted of fraud following a lengthy trial, and she faces up to twenty years in jail. The story caused a major stir in the USA because it lays bare one of the weak points of the entrepreneurial mentality shared by startuppers, the so-called "fake it till you make it" approach: first, to find investors, you promise extraordinary innovation; once you have the funds, you see if it is achievable. In recent years numerous companies have collapsed before their promises come to fruition or have revealed a disturbing dark side over time, to the point that *Fortune* has created an ironic scale to gauge the seriousness of a startupper's false promises, ranging from "Everyone does it" to "Time to hire new lawyers".

It's curious to note how Italians relate to this part of the world. It's not a well-known fact, but Italy is the only country in the G8 that doesn't have a journalist based in California (not a single person, not for the whole of the West Coast, from Canada all the way down to Mexico). Italian journalists prefer to be located in New York or, at a push, in Washington, DC. Thanks to the increasingly harsh cutbacks in the press and media, the result is that when something happens in San Francisco Italian journalists have to rush out there from New York on a budget flight, hire a car, have something explained to them by a local fixer or friend and then leave again. This, to a large degree, explains the dearth of knowledge about Northern California among the Italian public.

Also contributing to a lack of in-depth understanding is something known as "startup tourism", something a number of companies offer and which give aspiring startuppers a full-immersion experience of Silicon Valley. In just three days, a week at most, aspiring nerds will be shown the "Silicon Valley ecosystem", which will supposedly transform them for ever. It's a widespread phenomenon, and it's something you'll notice if you find yourself at one of the "sights" along the well-worn path that everyone takes when they head off to Silicon Valley – which nobody actually calls Silicon Valley, by the way, but "the Bay Area". (And *please* don't call San Francisco "Frisco".) Your itinerary will include a selection from the following: Facebook headquarters, the LinkedIn skyscraper in San Francisco and/or the Airbnb headquarters in SoMa (South of Market). You'll also be taken to see a few mysterious startups, complete with pimply kids in hoodies. Two places definitely on the itinerary include the famous garage in Palo Alto where Hewlett-Packard started and Steve Jobs's garage in Los Altos. Great photo ops. In truth, you quickly realise that the tour is really only good for ramping up your Instagram activity. Each stop has its own peculiarities: on the roof of the LinkedIn building is a huge sign constructed out of metal mesh that looks superb against the backdrop of the city skyline; Airbnb's headquarters has bedrooms named after cities around the world; Google has colourful bicycles.

All the headquarters of the large tech companies also have amazing cafeterias, each with their own specialities. LinkedIn, for example, has a popular ice cream shop upstairs, while downstairs is a fantastic salad bar. Airbnb's buffet also enjoys a strong reputation, as does the one at the Apple "spaceship" in Cupertino. Startup tourists can enjoy a delicious ice cream cone and leave happy. When the tour is over the sightseers will head home, diploma in hand, and will be able to tell their grandchildren that they experienced Silicon Valley in full when, in actual fact,

they were privy only to Instagrammable moments and the food.

While on one of these tours you come to realise that food has a surprising importance in Bay Area life, a fact you might never have expected. While Italians, like the French, generally consider themselves the undisputed authority on all things culinary, their Eurocentric certainties crumble when they travel to California. Generally speaking, people from the Mediterranean, Italy in particular, have an innate prejudice against the United States, particularly when it comes to food. When I decided to move to San Francisco my father commiserated with me. "Poor you," he said. "You'll become obese like the Americans who have nothing but hamburgers to eat."

Hence my surprise to find myself in a place where a) everyone is incredibly fit

A crowd in the showroom at Apple's Cupertino headquarters gathers to try out new products.

> **"In his fight against time and his illness, Steve Jobs not only wanted his new office in the 'spaceship' to be ready but he wanted the kitchen to be up and running, and it had to be under the management of an Italian chef."**

and b) there's not a McDonald's in sight. The level of a Californian's knowledge of food and culinary culture is surprising to an Italian. When I say I'm from Rome I expect the usual polite responses of "Oh Raphael, the pope, the Sistine Chapel", but in San Francisco someone once said to me, "Oh, Rome. It's so hard to find good food there." And it's true. Roman cuisine doesn't shine in terms of imagination and variety, at least not when compared with other regional Italian cuisines such as those of Naples or Sicily. The point is that it was an insider's remark – and a fact that most Italians don't even know.

Food is an obsession in the Bay Area. On the one hand it's part of a broader culture regarding the body. People stay fit thanks to the most disparate range of sports, they're always coming up with new food fads and diets (including superfoods, supplements and fasting), and then they're so damn "outdoorsy", a word that has become such an important adjective that you often find it mentioned on dating-app profiles as a prerequisite characteristic. On the other hand the Bay Area's understanding of food was greatly influenced by the hippie movement, whose members believed in living in close contact with nature, a way of life that is still a key part of California culture.

In his fight against time and his illness, Steve Jobs not only wanted his new office in the "spaceship" to be ready but he wanted the kitchen to be up and running, and it had to be under the management of an Italian chef. Peter Thiel, the legendary

founder of a number of tech empires, including PayPal, has an Italian chef who prepares mysterious concoctions for him based on seeds. (It is known that he intends to live for ever, or at least to the age of 120.) At one point, during a series of dinners for San Francisco startuppers and venture capitalists – an even more vital and prestigious category of people, henceforth VCs – I noticed that the people around me had started speaking in low voices as though they were confiding something to each other. I soon discovered that the hush-hush subject they were discussing had to do with bresaola. In the States, this Italian cured meat exists in something of a cloudy legal limbo, as it is neither raw nor cured. Clearly, though, it's a food favoured by startuppers and VCs, as they were sharing the name of an Italian who had set up a small bresaola production company somewhere near Sonoma with more enthusiasm, I gathered, than for certain ventures they were funding.

I, too, in my travels and reportage from the Bay Area, became – despite myself – something of a food correspondent. You realise quickly that food in the Bay Area is fundamental. I met and became friends with a few people who helped me understand the full implications of this. Fedele Bauccio, an eighty-year-old originally from southern Italy, is the founder of the Bon Appétit food-service company. This $1.5 billion company feeds everyone in the valley, providing food for the company cafeterias at Google, Oracle, Adobe, Uber, Yahoo, Twitter and LinkedIn. He also takes care of those at the headquarters of Disney, Amazon and Starbucks, not to mention Stanford University: 250 million meals a year, one thousand restaurants in thirty-four states. The son of a barber from Palermo and a Calabrian mother who emigrated to America, "Fedel" holds a degree in economics and can regularly be seen scooting around San Francisco on his red Vespa looking for steaks carved by a particular butcher, someone only he knows. Having started out as a dishwasher in a cafeteria at the University of Portland and going on to work in a catering company where he was shocked by the low quality of the food, he understood there was market potential. So he moved to Palo Alto with the intention of feeding the giants of the valley. The first to believe in him was Larry Ellison from Oracle, who asked him to set up a real Italian sandwich shop inside the company building. The rest is history.

Bauccio recognised the importance of organic ingredients and saw the notion of cooking dinner every night at home (or, worse, going out to restaurants) as being unsustainable for the Bay Area life-style: people liked to have lunch in their workplace cafeterias and bring home a snack, thereby saving money and time. So Bauccio focused on creating delicious meals for companies who use him (and his foods) as a draw for their employees, because, although money appears boun-tiful in this part of America, food is also a fundamental commodity and can be a precious asset for convincing the very best engineers or programmers to come and work for a particular company rather than the one next door. And in an ecosystem (such a Silicon Valley word) where companies compete to snap up the best employees, good (and free) food is one of the most prized benefits. There are even rankings: everyone knows that the food at Google, where Bauccio manages sixty restaurants for its sixty thousand employees, is the best. And then come all the others. Apple is the only company that charges its employees in its canteen. Bauccio also manages the two restaurants in the LinkedIn headquarters mentioned above: a salad bar on the thirteenth floor and a general restaurant on the third. (Streams of employees, as well as numerous gate-crashers, "check in" using a mysterious procedure that involves the omnipresent iPad and printing out a label that you then stick on yourself.)

The second person who helped me understand California food culture is Alice Waters, the legendary founder of the Chez Panisse restaurant in Berkeley. She's the one who convinced the Obamas to plant a real organic garden at the White House (the Clintons only had a small tomato patch on the roof) and to offer a simple peach as dessert to an astonished Bill Clinton, a renowned gourmand. It was a political gesture. Waters has always been a champion of local organic food and is involved in the fight to offer healthy food to school kids; her Edible Schoolyard Project aims to connect educational insti-tutions with farms so that students can eat fresh, wholesome food while providing farmers with sustainable business. Her restaurant, which has been in the same location for over fifty years (it opened in 1971), has served everyone from Black Panthers to techies, surviving all the changes in the Bay Area, and she's still there, still talking about healthy foods, still making it a question of politics in a country where so many people still eat lunch in their cars or in front of the TV. And, although the counterculture might be over and the terrorists gone, a "gourmet ghetto" thrives in and around Berkeley, creating a kind of rarefied

Decades of zero tolerance had not only reduced the public's desire to experiment with but also the scientific community's interest in studying the psychotropic substances that became popular in the wake of 1967's Summer of Love. But the field is now the subject of renewed curiosity on medical, recreational and spiritual levels – and California is, of course, at the forefront. Oakland was the first US city to decriminalise psychedelics such as hallucinogenic mushrooms and ayahuasca, followed by Denver, Colorado, and there are now also discussions at state level, with a grassroots movement collecting signatures for a referendum. A bill has also been submitted by Senator Scott Wiener to regulate the possession of small quantities of psilocybin, psilocin, ecstasy, LSD, DMT, mescaline (excluding peyote) and ibogaine. These political moves reflect a rethinking of psychoactive substances hinging on their benefits in the treatment of conditions such as depression and anxiety, which have worsened during the pandemic. But the psychedelic renaissance is also a social phenomenon: every weekend dozens of ayahuasca ceremonies are held in the great outdoors, shamans travel back and forth from Brazil and Peru to perform the ceremonies in locations such as Topanga Canyon, companies with names like My Ketamine Home organise group sessions and there is even a 24/7 telephone hotline offering information for safer tripping. This is a revolution driven by an unusual marriage of science and spirituality, between those who are investigating the therapeutic effects of psychedelics and those who believe they will put humanity on a path to a spiritual awakening.

district around Chez Panisse. And it's not just about food. There's ample room for a host of thinkers, too: Stanford superstar and founding director of the Center on Food Security and the Environment Roz Naylor; essayist Michael Pollan, the author of *Cooked*, possibly the most important book in recent years on the subject of food, as well as a scholar of the effects of different substances on the human organism (after his foray into food, he delved into psychotropic substances); and let's not forget farm-labour activist Eric Holt Giménez as well as several other local academics, culinary experts and technologists all intent on examining how we eat.

Also at Berkeley is Judith Butler, who directs the critical theory programme. She is the godmother of the gender theory that drives the conservative media across the world nuts, convinced as they are that the "dictatorship of the politically correct" is upon us, while the truth is that in France or Italy importing intersectionality and the precepts of everything PC is proving much harder than introducing avocado toast and the iPhone. In those countries public debate is fierce, traditional and colourful; you hear all kinds of insults, both in parliament and the newspapers. Black female MPs are sometimes referred to by the kinds of epithets that would never be heard these days in public life in the USA, and no one is ever sanctioned for it. Comedians in top-rated programmes on state-run TV complain about not being allowed to use derogatory terms to speak about minorities any longer, and yet public opinion would have us believe that the "thought police" are on patrol. While political correctness has existed in the United States for forty years, it is still taking baby steps in Italy and having a hard time of it. And then there's the #MeToo movement. It's good to recall that this, too, was born in Silicon Valley and only later did it roll downhill to Hollywood. It all started in early 2017 when Susan Fowler, an Uber employee, wrote a post – which later grew into a well-known book, *Whistleblower: My Journey to Silicon Valley and Fight for Justice at Uber* (Penguin, 2021) – in which she denounced the discrimination she suffered within the company responsible for wiping taxis off the face of the earth. This all seems very abstract and futuristic to us in Italy; the few actresses who have complained about disrespectful directors were quickly silenced, and everything was buried. (A friend of mine says that Italy is where the #MeToo movement comes to die.) So while in California the campus left raises fears of radicalism, in Italy our university rectors (straight white men – the sons and grandsons of past rectors) now feel threatened by the remote hint of that "dictatorship of political correctness".

Going back to Uber, I recall how Alice Waters once said to me in Rome, "How nice to see you have taxis again, that you've abolished Uber. Bravo." (In Northern California Uber is seen as a dangerous company that represents the worst of the patriarchy following stories of harassment around its founder and its corporate culture.) It was embarrassing to have to explain to Waters that Uber never actually made it to Italy, at least not in its widespread American form, and that taxis still have a monopoly here.

Actually, this reminds me of something I've been mulling over for some time. Generally speaking, we live in an era where everyone seems to be in the same time zone – due in large part to social media and global TV series – but in many ways there's still an enormous gap, a kind of cultural time zone, between the USA's more evolved areas (the Bay Area, *in primis*) and the rest of the world. For better or worse, American society changes rapidly; for better or worse, changes in many European countries happen very slowly. And that's why we love them so. We are a slow people, we cultivate traditions, and in a number of ways we still seem to have something of a 1950s lifestyle. And yet we continue to pretend we all exist in the same time zone. That's why the prejudices that a citizen of one country projects on to another are so interesting. That's why it's so fascinating to perceive how customs and traditions are transmitted and modified. Imagine you're an Italian and you step into a café in the Mission District, that once run-down but now very gentrified San Francisco neighbourhood, and you order an espresso. The tattoo-covered barista (note the Italian word) sets a small timer and calculates how long the infusion will take, with the result being a green beverage that has a decidedly sour taste. When you complain, the barista says, "That's how it's done in Italy!" And there's no convincing him otherwise, that espresso in Italian means fast, on the fly. The barista sees that kind of coffee as being Italian, end of story.

The history of coffee in San Francisco offers another interesting example of how recipes and national identities are transmitted. Before greenish "local", "sustainable" coffee came along (also known as "gourmet" coffee and often found in fruity or "fermented" versions), there was a glut of low-quality raw material, which can still be found here and there. The second

SILICON BEACH

While the Bay Area has its Silicon Valley, Los Angeles has its Silicon Beach, the city's technology district – even though no microchips are produced there, so there's no whiff of actual silicon. And if truth be told, it's not strictly accurate to describe the entire area as a beach; the name refers to an area of LA's Westside that includes Malibu, Santa Monica and Venice but also Culver City inland. The "beach" is home to the headquarters of more than five hundred technology firms, and the area received a significant boost in 2018 when Google, Apple and Facebook opened huge offices there. The birth of Silicon Beach dates back to the early 2010s, when some early startups, such as Snapchat and Tinder, were established. Today, also thanks to new graduates from Caltech, it is a development hub above all

for the entertainment sector (it was the birthplace of Hulu, and Netflix and YouTube have also recently opened offices there); as the internet is dominated by the smartphone, and video accounts for an ever-greater share of content, the proximity of Hollywood and a tradition of video games (Riot Games is based in LA) has proved to be strategically advantageous. Most of the capital remains in the Bay Area, however, and the result has been a bizarre rise in commuting by private jet (for CEOs, obviously) with a consequent growth in that market – it is no coincidence that Silicon Beach's development began with the airport. This long-distance capitalism makes it more difficult for companies to grow, which also has some positive effects: the lower budgets force entrepreneurs to look for more creative solutions to problems while taking greater care of (and listening more closely to) their customers.

wave, an imitation of Italian coffee, was born in San Francisco thanks to a Dutch gentleman named Alfred Peet, who opened his first coffee shop in Berkeley in 1966 and enjoyed astonishing success. Peet's was everywhere. One of the people who regularly drank Peet's coffee was a student named Howard Schultz, who built Starbuck's into a global brand. The coffee from that second phase was decent in quality but too heavily roasted, and the result was a burnt-tasting hot beverage that Americans loaded with milk and sugar to ameliorate its bitterness.

Today, if you put sugar in your coffee in San Francisco, someone will call the cops. We're in the third wave now. This is the gourmet version, the hipster phase, where tattooed baristas take half an hour to make green coffee that can only be further diluted with soya milk. Look at the case of Blue Bottle, a local company that now has a hundred or so outlets around the world. It's a classic tale: a clarinet player drops out of music school,

Taking a selfie in front of the Facebook sign at the company's headquarters in Menlo Park.

starts a coffee business and then retires. This tart, green, gourmet drink, which Americans think of as Italian will, five years down the road, eventually make its way to Italy. And we shall see then what Italians think of it ...

But it's not just food crazes that eventually make their way back to the Old World; revolutions and innovations in personal habits travel, too. Just a few miles south of San Francisco, in Foster City, lies the pharmaceutical giant Gilead. In 2012 this company introduced Truvada to the market, a drug better known as PrEP (pre-exposure prophylaxis). This pill has revolutionised sex across the globe for gay people and heterosexuals alike. Now being used by a growing number of people, the nemesis of Aids was born in the same city that was the epicentre of the crisis back in the 1980s and 1990s. The drug has done away with condom culture and is bringing sex back to the way it was before the epidemic, before the notion of "gay sex = death" and the consequent moral obligation to use condoms.

PrEP is a fantastic blend of a number of aspects typical of the Bay Area: the cult of the body and physical wellbeing, the pleasure principle and a love of money. And let's not forget gay culture, which is yet another important substratum of this city. San Francisco has been an outpost for queer culture for the past two hundred years. Initially, it was a place of confinement (like certain remote Italian islands) for homosexuals serving in the navy who managed to get caught. Then, as the city grew after 1848 (following the discovery of gold and the subsequent Gold Rush), it attracted increasingly large numbers of men (with strong arms to work in the mines). Two centuries ago the first gay bars were located in the Barbary Coast port district (now unrecognisable) and were much like the saloon in which Clark Gable runs his bar in the 1936 film *San Francisco*. The demographics have always been unbalanced – too many men, too few women – to the extent that at one point the city imported ten thousand prostitutes from wherever they could find them just to balance things out. Even so, by the end of the 19th century Oscar Wilde enthusiastically stated that he had never been to a queerer city. Things continued to develop in the 20th century when the Castro District became the gay epicentre of America and the world. (The Castro is home to a museum dedicated to Harvey Milk, the legendary city councilman and first openly gay official who was assassinated with Mayor George Moscone, after whom the Moscone Center is named, that mythical convention centre where Apple products were once presented before Jobs built his big ring.) In 1964 *Life* magazine officially stated that San Francisco was the gay capital of America (what fun it must have been, with the saunas, cruising and the Summer of Love). Then, in the 1980s the epidemic arrived. Today, thanks to this blue pill which will one day hopefully become a vaccine (it relies on the same mRNA biomechanics as anti-Covid vaccines) there's a chance that life will be able to go properly back to normal.

This big blue pill reduces people's chances of infection by 99 per cent, and, like that other blue pill, it is rapidly changing global habits, in this case allowing people to go back to pre-HIV/Aids hedonistic activities. Condoms have since become bizarre, retro objects that people talk about in chat rooms the way you'd hear people refer to VHS tapes or faxes. "Condoms? Um, no thanks." The social implications of this medicine are dramatic: not only will people stop developing Aids but those who have it will stop being marginalised, effectively rehabilitating a much-abused section of the population.

PrEP has arrived in Europe and is slowly but surely spreading. Will young Italians who take it know that it comes from California and Silicon Valley? Maybe they'll get confused with that other Prep – that famous brand of shaving cream that has been available in Italy since 1860, a symbol of old-school virility, our grandparents' kind, and which is still sold in Italian supermarkets. Actually, you can even find the shaving cream in some of the hippest barber shops in San Francisco, such as Fellow Barber on Valencia Street. Who knows what a Californian might think if they see the two Prep products standing next to each other. Luckily, one is in tablet form and the other is a cream. Mixing them up could seriously damage your health. ✐

Gone:
The Burning
of Paradise

MARK ARAX

Photographs by Josh Edelson

Firefighters demolish a wall while fighting the flames at an apartment complex in Paradise. More than ten thousand homes, a hospital and many other buildings in the area were destroyed.

A distinguished investigative reporter tells the terrifying story of the 2018 Paradise fire, in which eighty-five people died and thousands of homes were destroyed, explaining why it should never have happened but will happen again and why climate change is not the single most significant factor.

127

By the time I made it to Paradise, the deadliest wildfire in California history was four months past, and the burned-out ridge between the two river canyons was pouring rain. I was riding the Skyway, the road from Chico to Paradise, flatland to hilltop, trying to understand what forces had conspired the previous November to create a blaze of such anger that it took the lives of eighty-five people and destroyed nineteen thousand structures.

I had puzzled out enough disasters to know that tragedy was a force of intricate construction. It wasn't one detached act that materialized as tragedy but myriad smaller acts—some incidental, some accidental, others malevolent—that lined up in perfect continuity. Had one circumstance in the sequence lost its footing, a cosmic stumble, the next circumstance would have never hitched on, and tragedy would have been averted.

Halfway into the ridge, the black clouds cleared and the rain stopped falling. Through the ponderosa pine and cedar, the sun shot brilliant rays that lit up both sides of the Skyway. The extent of the fire's destruction now became clear. My tour guide, Joan Degischer, a native of Paradise who married a Paradise boy and was raising two Paradise girls, counted six houses in her extended family that had been lost to the fire. As she drove from one ravaged spot to the next, she seemed unsure whether to narrate the ruin herself or keep quiet so that the visitor might find his own words.

On this perch of volcanic red earth, where gold mining gave way to logging and logging gave way to apple growing and apple growing gave way to suburbia, a misplaced place had arisen. What to call the experiment? If you counted the sprawl up the mountain that followed the original sprawl on the hill, forty thousand people lived atop a geological chimney. Although the citizens through the decades were unable to muster the collective will to contain the growth, they did not proceed out of ignorance of the dangers it courted. Rather, they chose to forget about the last drought, the last flood, the last wildfire. And so, self-consciously, as if it might save them from such a fate, they insisted Paradise wasn't a "city" they were building on the ridge. It was, upon

MARK ARAX is a journalist and writer who grew up in a Central Valley farming family, and he has spent his working life reporting on his home state of California. His style has been compared with that of William Saroyan and the great social portraits of Joan Didion. His biography of J.G. Boswell, the greatest agricultural entrepreneur in US history, *The King of California: J.G. Boswell and the Making of a Secret American Empire* (PublicAffairs, 2005), won a California Book Award and the William Saroyan prize. His most recent title, *The Dreamt Land: Chasing Water and Dust Across California* (Knopf, 2019), which also garnered a California Book Award, investigates the history of land and water use and misuse in California.

incorporation in 1979, an official town. The Town of Paradise. The "town with a future" went the slogan.

It was empty now, and it was filled up. Scorched trees and felled trees, burned shells of cars and melted piles of twisted corrugated tin, ashes of businesses, ashes of houses, ashes of people had become its own place. There were stretches of the Skyway where fire had not touched what the townsfolk had built, but these stretches had been altered, too, turned into things no longer recognizable by the things that were missing. Brick chimneys stood guard over the voids like giant middle fingers.

We could only speak to what was gone:

Jack in the Box ... gone.
Century 21... gone.
Edward Jones Investments ... gone.
Kelly's Muffler ... gone.
The Skyway Antique Mall ... gone.
The Safeway Shopping Center ... gone.
The Paradise Inn and Momma Celeste's
  pizzeria ... gone.
Evergreen Mobile Home Park and the
  Newton-Bracewell Crematorium ...
  gone.

Degischer turned on to Camellia Drive and tried to find familiar ground. The Feather River had gouged out the canyon to our left; Butte Creek had gouged out the canyon to our right. A half-dozen longtime families had once lived on the crooked little street. Their houses were made of wood, she said, and their gardens were painted with flowers. The Parrots, the Yermans, the Mackays, the Woods. Harvey Parrot was a popular dentist in town. His daughter married a dentist named Chatfield, and they lived on Camellia, too. A retired female professor from UC Berkeley moved in next door.

SANTA ANA WINDS

A flow of air from the desert to the north-east, sucked in by low pressure on the Southern Californian plain, blows over the Sierra Nevada, gains speed as it threads through the ravines of the Santa Ana Canyon and the Cajon Pass, then rushes downhill with the power of a storm (sometimes in excess of 170 km/h), growing a degree hotter for every 100-metre drop (it can reach up to 40 degrees Celsius). The phenomenon occurs in Los Angeles particularly in the autumn when the Santa Ana winds blow, sometimes with devastating consequences, particularly if the area has already been suffering a prolonged drought. It only takes a spark to set off a fire, and at this point the wind fuels the spread of California's wildfires while making them more unpredictable and uncontrollable. But it does not only affect the environment: "To live with the Santa Ana is to accept, consciously or unconsciously, a deeply mechanistic view of human behavior," wrote Joan Didion in her essay "Los Angeles Notebook". On the days when it blows people are more irritable, if not downright hot-headed, because the wind also seems to affect the human psyche, filling the air with sand, heat and an exhausting tension. This is the same *Red Wind* that provided the title for a story by the noir writer Raymond Chandler, who claimed that on Santa Ana nights, "anything can happen". Even the name has disturbing overtones. An innocuous reference to the place where the wind often originates, a canyon some fifty kilometres from Los Angeles, it could also derive from the similar-sounding Spanish word Satana. For the avoidance of doubt, it is also known in California as the Devil (or Diablo) Wind.

> **"'We're in the middle of town,' he'd say. 'All these structures surround us. For a fire to get to Camellia Drive, it would have to be Armageddon.'"**

All the previous canyon fires, including a blaze that raced up the ridgeline in June 2008 and consumed seventy-four houses, had let this neighborhood be. But the orange-red tornado that came down the Feather canyon at 7 a.m. on the morning of 8 November 2018, was riding sixty-five mph (105 km/h) winds. Only a single house, the one belonging to the professor, was left standing.

Degischer pulled up to one of the voids. "This is where I grew up," she said. What she said next sounded like testimony. "My parents are Michael and Debra Wood. We moved into this house in 1989, when I was one year old. My brother Jack was born here. It was 1,700 square feet on a full acre [160 square meters on half a hectare]. There used to be a rose garden over there. We stood in front of it for our prom and graduation pictures. We had a peach tree, a walnut tree, and a Chinese pistache tree that was everyone's favorite because it turned bright red and orange."

Her mom was a hippie from Oakland, and her dad was a local boy, and their politics both leaned liberal, which made for a rare upbringing on the ridge. They gave her and her four siblings plenty of room to roam and passed on a love of Led Zeppelin and Merle Haggard, the latter allowing her some cred with the local rednecks. "I was a *Star Wars* geek growing up," she said. "Still am."

She and her husband Kyle had come back to Paradise after college to raise their two daughters. She took a job as an office assistant at Cedarwood Elementary.

Kyle was a respiratory therapist who worked half the week out of town. Their eldest daughter, Freya, was about to turn eight. Degischer had named her after the goddess of Norse mythology. Tamzin, short for Thomasina, was four and sitting in the back seat. She had been born with cerebral palsy and was growing more impatient with each stop. Her mother was a study in calm, conjuring one distraction after another trying to soothe her. Mint candies finally did the trick.

Their own house, nestled on the upper ridge, had survived the fire. This was maybe her tenth time back to the house where she grew up. Each visit she found herself without the need to dig her knees into the ash. She wasn't like her family and friends who sifted and sifted through the remains, a compulsion she understood. Each time their eyes caught a glint of something, they'd shout "Look here" and pick it up like it was a shred of proof. They would hold it in their hands only for it to disintegrate and be gone, too.

Her mother had stored their history in the master-bedroom closet and the garage rafters. Not a thing of it was left. Not the high-school yearbooks or wedding albums or the knickknacks handed down

A shop burns in Paradise (**top**), while (**bottom**) survivors search through what's left of their home.

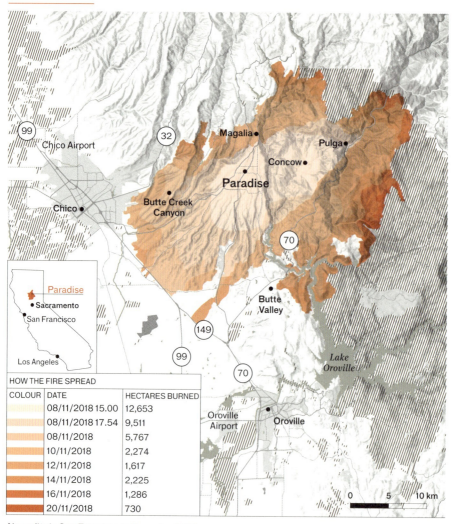

HOW THE FIRE SPREAD

COLOUR	DATE	HECTARES BURNED
	08/11/2018 15.00	12,653
	08/11/2018 17.54	9,511
	08/11/2018	5,767
	10/11/2018	2,274
	12/11/2018	1,617
	14/11/2018	2,225
	16/11/2018	1,286
	20/11/2018	730

Air quality in San Francisco in November 2018

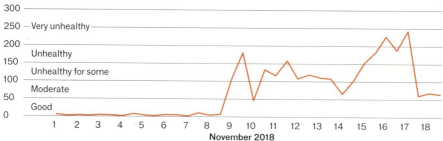

SOURCE: REDZONE AND WIKIPEDIA

the generations. Degischer had to call an old friend to recover a wallet-sized version of her high-school graduation photo. As a kid, she had fears of such a fire, and her father would tell her not to worry. "'We're in the middle of town,' he'd say. 'All these structures surround us. For a fire to get to Camellia Drive, it would have to be Armageddon.'"

She steered past the professor's house into a larger void where the sunlight seemed cruel. Then she caught sight of the rest of the neighborhood as the street made its bend. It was a cliché, she knew, *the phoenix rising from the ashes*, but there up ahead, out of the soot, a camellia bush stood in full bloom.

She showed me the grocery store where her father worked as a clerk; the dive bar that served Chinese food where her mom was a waitress; the house where her grandfather Jack, a local prosecutor who had fled the Dust Bowl, lived; the day-care center where she landed her first job; and the Round Table Pizza where her husband learned to sling dough. Each place had been taken by fire. "I've been through it dozens of times," she said, "but it never quite sinks in. 'What even happened?' I ask myself."

The blaze had not altered her belief that the ridge—its seclusion and familiarity, its comfort and kinship—was a fine place to raise their children. As she drove back up the hill to where my car was parked, I wondered aloud about the wisdom of building a town where the risk to life and home was so great. "Did fire come to Paradise, or did Paradise go to the fire?" I asked.

She nodded and considered an answer. Her pause made me think that my question—the facile either/or of it—wasn't fair. To someone still absorbing the dimensions of what had taken place

here, it might even have been cruel. She could have told me to go to hell, and I would have understood. Before she could answer, I made a brushing motion with my left hand and swept the question away. The answer wasn't so simple, I offered. Besides, the answer was mine to figure out. She nodded again.

*

It starts—where else?—with men digging. Not the digging by the Maidu people, whose ten thousand years on the ridge hardly left a notch, but by the Americans who came at it with claws.

The year was 1859, and all the easy gold had been fished out of the Feather and Butte Creek. In nearby Dogtown, a forty-niner named Chauncey Wright unearthed a record 54-pound (24.5-kilogram) nugget worth $10,690. He wasn't using pan and pickax. Hydraulic mining, bending water into flumes and pressurizing it through hoses with nozzles, found his nugget. The rivers and canyons now belonged to industrialists who lived on San Francisco's Nob Hill and possessed the capital to erect a sprawling system to capture and convey water.

Up the ridge rode William Leonard and his wagon crew in the wicked summer of 1860. He grabbed the shade of a ponderosa pine, the air light and cool, unlike any other he had ever breathed. "Boys," he said, "this has got to be paradise." This was as good a guess as any for how the town earned its name. Lumber was the new gold, he preached. He built a sawmill and a road that connected the ridge to the valley below. A church, a post office, John Strong's General Store, and a Southern Pacific depot followed.

By 1902, the Diamond Match Company had acquired 55,000 acres (22,260 hectares) on the ridge and built an even bigger sawmill that sent lumber down to Chico where the matches were made. Two powerhouses were turning river flow into electricity. The new Pacific Gas and Electric Company (PG&E), formed in 1905 with the merger of two smaller utilities in San Francisco and already gaining a reputation as a water-sucking serpent, made a play to own the ridge's power. It bought the dam and reservoir the people had built and erected a new distribution system.

The early settlers had fled to the hills to get away from government, but they buried their suspicions long enough to form the Paradise Irrigation District in 1916. Irrigation domesticated, if not tamed, the ridge. Twelve thousand acres (five thousand hectares) of pears, walnuts, olives, grapes, and apples were planted in the red soil. Heinke's organic apple juice—made from "ripe, sound, washed, unsprayed mountain apples"—was prized throughout the state.

Chico looked up the mountain and down its nose at Paradise, which the flatlanders called "Poverty Ridge." Only fifteen miles (twenty-four kilometers) separated the two communities, but the houses in Paradise were much cheaper. If a mobile-home park was the only dwelling you could afford, Paradise offered scores of open spaces under the pines. Poor white folk flocked to the ridge to beat the heat in summer and the tule fog in winter. Paradise soon found itself battling Chico for the right to run its own school district, even as its elementary school kept burning down.

By 1953, the Skyway had been paved and then expanded. The number of businesses grew 50 per cent in a six-year span. As the population swelled to ten thousand, including large contingents of Mormons and Seventh-day Adventists, the growth might well have slowed or stopped, considering the ridge's potential for wind-blown wildfire. But the forests of California were a new frontier, a place to celebrate the Western itch of reinvention and forever expansion. A boom was on, and neither the state nor the county dared dictate to Paradise what it should or shouldn't be.

Pam Figge, an exile from Glendale fleeing the freeway life, moved to Paradise in the go-go year of 1971. She signed up for classes at Chico State and went to work at the weekly *Ridge Gazette*, covering the Planning Commission and Board of Supervisors. "When it came to developing Paradise, it was anything goes. The loudest citizens wanted no governance, and the supervisors were more than happy to comply," she said.

The first time Figge heard the term "four-by-fouring" in the county planning office, she wasn't sure what it meant. A businessman bought a parcel in Paradise, and supervisors promptly agreed to his request to divide the parcel into four pieces. Then, he sold one of the pieces to a partner, who went before the same board and won approval to divide his piece into four. On and on the slicing and dicing went. The number four wasn't arbitrary. Had they split each piece into five, it would have qualified as a "subdivision" under state law and required developers and residents to fund the proper infrastructure to serve such growth.

Instead, scores of housing tracts popped up without sidewalks or gutters or buffers to provide a defensible space against fire. Roads came later, if they came at all. A municipal sewage system was never constructed. Septic tanks made of concrete—or nothing more than redwood planks covering a hole filled with gravel—handled the chore. You could smell the human waste bubbling

As if fires and drought were not enough, California also has another climate-change-related problem: rising sea levels. Its coastline developments grew during a period in which the Pacific was unusually benevolent, making it possible to build next to the ocean. Things are changing, however, and the water could rise by over two metres by the end of this century. The problems are already evident: cliffs collapsing and sending the houses built on them crashing into the ocean (as in the town of Pacifica); islands forced to build huge and extremely expensive flood defences so as not to be submerged (like Balboa Island); winter storms destroying the seafront boardwalk (as happened at Capistrano Beach). The solution typically supported by homeowners has so far consisted of building barriers and breakwaters, but these are costly to put in and to maintain, and many places lack the resources. Every barrier also effectively means giving up on the beach, which can no longer renew itself naturally, so it becomes a race against time to import sand from elsewhere (and the supply of sand is neither infinite nor inexpensive). People have started to talk about a managed retreat, in other words pulling back and giving up space to nature, but the concept is impossible to sell to owners and goes against the American mentality: you don't withdraw, you defend. The few brave mayors who have proposed the idea have been punished by their electorates. Ultimately, though, no means of defence is painless or cheap, and in local councils the discussions between environmentalists, real-estate developers, administrators and officials from the Coastal Commission are growing ever more heated.

up in the earth. "At some point, the septic tanks started failing, and Paradise had to say 'No' to any more restaurants or laundries," Figge said. "There wasn't enough capacity to handle their waste."

So what does a place bred to grow but hemmed in by two canyons do? It goes higher up the narrow ridge and plants a new upscale community called Paradise Pines and markets it to retirees. Lured by newspaper ads in San Francisco and TV spots across the state, they arrived by the thousands in the 1960s and 1970s. They carted their equity and, in some cases, liberal politics to Paradise Pines and another growing burg nearby called Magalia. Poverty Ridge wasn't so impoverished any more. Rednecks, retirees, and hippies could agree on this much: no arm of the local or state government need lay a hand on their pine trees.

After years of wrangling, the residents had decided to make it official and declare themselves an incorporated town. They elected a mayor and four town council members who ran on the same slate—the "Qualified Five." No sooner were they sworn into office than they fired the town manager, planning director, and police chief.

As much as Paradise wanted to steer its own fate, the Qualified Five were nervous about the prospect that the town's first general plan would bring new bureaucrats, new regulations, new taxes, and maybe even a sewer system to the ridge. Years of ugly recall elections—recalls all the way down to the Irrigation District Board—followed. Those who wanted no government feuded with those who wanted some and those who wanted more. One spunky elderly couple, Wilson and Mona Locke, got so fed up with seeing more houses added pell-mell to the forest that they sued Paradise in 1998 for its refusal to require

> "The Indians gave us the natural forest. Much of it was patchy, and the trees grew to differing heights. This combination of open ground and uneven canopy kept the fires from raging."

sewers and roads to escape fire. Because of their objections, the Saddleback Canyon Estates subdivision never took ground. But even as the town was forced to hire a professional staff of planners and more or less follow a set of regulations and zoning codes, it was too late: thirty thousand residents were now living in the suburban equivalent of a tinderbox.

When the first of the big fires swept the foothills of Butte County in the summer of 2008, sixty thousand acres (twenty-four thousand hectares) burned and seventy-four houses were lost or heavily damaged on the edge of Paradise. By some twist, the flames did not cross the west branch of the Feather River and leap over to the Skyway. The smoke alone closed three of the four major evacuation routes from Paradise and Magalia. In the fire's wake, the county grand jury issued a report asking questions that no state or local agency had ever asked of the Town Council or the Board of Supervisors. How was it that no assessment district had ever been formed on the ridge to levy fees in the name of fire safety? How was it that the main emergency route out of Paradise was lined with a thicket of pine trees and brush? How was it that the county's new draft of the 2030 general plan barely addressed fire risk and fire safety? And how was it that the general plan was looking to put 3,400 more houses and fifteen thousand more people in the same path of deadly wildfire?

*

I left the ridge and headed deeper into the woodlands of California, clutching a remarkable book called *Fire in Sierra Nevada Forests*, written in 2001 by wildlife biologist George Gruell, which documents the ecological changes to the mountain range since Chauncey Wright discovered his rock of gold. The photos date back as far as 1849 and depict great swaths of the Sierra with only a scattering of trees. The forest looks strangely forlorn. More than a century and a half later, these same locations reveal an entirely different Sierra. What was once sparse is now densely packed with pine, fir, cedar, and manzanita. A forest that supported sixty-four trees an acre in pre-settlement times now boasted 160 trees an acre. The modern eye sees this mountain-to-mountain vegetation as proof of the forest's good health. Like the border-to-border almond trees in the valley below, vigor would appear to be nature at its most eloquent. But that is not what nature intended. "The landscapes of today may look attractively lush," Gruell writes, "but the thickening forest threatens us with several problems."

I thought I might find the spiritual progeny of John Muir, the Scot who regarded the mountain as a temple and could speak to the manifold ways we've screwed up the forest and complicated human existence in a place that, quite independent of global climate change, delivers its own violent fits of nature. I found instead Richard Wilson, an old cattleman who ran the California

THE PASSENGER   Mark Arax

Department of Forestry and Fire Protection in the 1990s.

He lived alone on Buck Mountain across the Eel River deep in the Mendocino woods, surrounded by pot growers. Years before, he had led the fight to defeat the massive dam that state bureaucrats wanted to build on the Eel to send more irrigation water to the cotton kings in Fresno; he had done battle with the timber barons, too, although he wasn't able to stop the madness of their clear-cutting. And now he was closing in on eighty-six years old and never more cantankerous, bull-headed and opinionated, or at least that was the view of his rancher son, who lived on his own remote spread an hour away. The elder Wilson wasn't the second coming of Muir, but after sixty years as a heretic on his mountain, he was close enough.

"I don't think we could have managed the forests any worse," he told me by way of greeting. His voice was strained, but he was still sturdy and rawboned, and only recently had his full head of hair gone to gray. Back in 1972, when he stood next to Governor Ronald Reagan to celebrate the state law that would protect the Eel, Wilson was the one who looked like the movie star. After a lifetime fighting battles both here and in Sacramento, he was feeling worn out, he said, but one cause still roused him each morning: a saner and safer way of treating the forest.

"The Indians gave us the natural forest. Much of it was patchy, and the trees grew to differing heights," he said. "This combination of open ground and uneven canopy kept the fires from raging. Now the fires are raging. They're racing from forest to suburbia, and we're scratching our heads trying to figure out why. Remember, fire is a natural event in a healthy forest. It starts by lightning strike and usually burns itself out quickly. But before it does, it scorches the forest floor and thins out lower branches and shrubs. This helps tame the next fire. This allows new trees to generate. The timber companies could have worked inside that natural cycle and harvested a sustainable amount of wood. Instead, they were allowed to clear-cut the old growth and plant new trees one on top of the other."

He was talking about how industrialized agriculture had come to the mountain. "So the trees are just another crop?" I asked.

"That's right," he said. "The growth is so uniform that when fire hits it, it becomes a blowtorch. The trees are nothing but matchsticks. Get a spark up, and she's gone."

"You're saying we've turned our forest into easy kindling. But what about the kindling of man's settlement?" I asked.

"Even though I was the head of state Forestry and Fire, I couldn't stop it. When I left the agency, I wrote that these were 'unprecedented patterns of human settlement' in areas that John Muir had called 'God's wildness.' The settlement patterns resulted in perhaps the most rapid and massive disruption of natural fire regimes and watersheds ever experienced on earth."

From 1990 to 2010, the number of houses built in the wildland–urban interface grew by a million in California. The number of people rose by nearly three million. One out of every four Californians—more than ten million people—now lived in the zone of wildfire. They were scattered across Butte, Shasta, Contra Costa, Alameda, and San Luis Obispo counties. More than half resided in Los Angeles, Riverside, San Bernardino, Orange, and San Diego counties. The 2020 census shows a new protrusion of growth

THE PASSENGER   Mark Arax

Opposite top: Patients are evacuated from Feather River Hospital, which was caught up in the fire.
Opposite bottom: A deer stands in the wreckage of a house in Paradise.

in the path of peril, even as six of the ten most destructive wildfires in state history have taken place since 2010.

Wilson's old department remained as powerless as ever to stop suburbia's march on the woodlands. Climate change or not, the state of California continued to exercise almost no voice in county land-use decisions. The most the fire agency could muster was that locals "should" include a consideration of fire danger when approving growth. Then something happened inside the agency that was even more telling, Wilson said. The department responded to the expanding footprint of risk by expanding right along with it. Today, it calls itself what it has become: Cal Fire. The khaki uniforms of the old forestry days were gone. The flat-brim hats were long gone, too. The men and women of Cal Fire now wore the navy blue of firefighters everywhere in the US.

The change happened right after Wilson left Sacramento in 1999 to return to Buck Mountain. It wasn't simply a shift in colors. It was a shift in mission. Firefighters on the front lines of a blaze had grown tired of taking orders from forestry rangers who had less experience but a more lofty ranking. This hierarchy was the result of an old policy that placed a premium on managing the forest and preventing wildfires. The firefighters, boasting a new ethic, formed their own union, Local 2881, and bargained for

their own workweek: seventy-two hours over a three-day period with a compensation package far more lucrative than the foresters'. Rangers soon found themselves second-class citizens in a department they once commanded. The services they performed—coordinating prescribed burns, protecting watersheds from the wrack of clear-cuts, reducing so-called fuel loads in mountain communities—were curtailed. As rangers joined up with the ranks of better-paid firefighters, their numbers dwindled to maybe 250, even as the number of firefighters inside the department jumped to seven thousand.

By the early 2000s, the structuring of California firefighting into a disaster-industrial complex—the deification of "first responders," as they became known in the wake of 9/11—had been fully realized. Today, the war-like mobilization of firefighting is nothing if not epic. Each battle required air tankers, helicopters, bulldozers, all-terrain fire engines, thousands of firefighters and inmate conservation workers, hundreds of fire stations, and a statewide communications system. "Fire suppression" was now a $1.1 billion line item in the department's budget—a new record. And this didn't fully include the $300 million for a dozen new Black Hawk helicopters to replace the fleet of Vietnam-era Hueys needed to transport fire crews in and out of steep terrain.

As I ticked off the costs of the Black Hawks and the seven C-130 Hercules cargo planes that would be retrofitted to each carry up to four thousand US gallons (fifteen thousand liters) of flame retardant, Wilson reminded me that fighting wildfires is chiefly a summer-to-fall occupation. To justify its high costs, the department had to figure out a way to make itself essential throughout the year. This was how it evolved into a 24/7 provider of emergency services to the sprawling mountain communities. Cal Fire manned fire stations throughout the wildland–urban interface. The paramedics responding to heart attacks wore Cal Fire patches on their blue. In other words, the department existed as a partner with towns such as Paradise. Instead of trying to slow down the suburbanization of forestlands, Wilson said, the department served the growth—to the tune of hundreds of millions of dollars a year in funding.

"It's a money maker," Wilson said. "When it came to growth, the department and the state of California held back their criticism. And we've made wrong turn after wrong turn. What happened to Paradise is the culmination of the errors of our ways."

*

During my first visit to Paradise, Joan Degischer remembered getting a phone call from PG&E on 7 November, the evening before the fire. The short recorded message advised her that power to the ridge would likely be shut off the next day. In the wake of a five-year drought that had killed tens of millions of trees in the Sierra, the weather forecast was predicting low humidity and winds gusting to fifty mph (eighty km/h)—perfect wildfire conditions.

As a precaution against "increasing fire risk," PG&E had activated its Emergency Operations Center on 6 November, and over the next two days directed multiple phone calls, emails, text messages, and press releases to tens of thousands of customers. Across Butte County and eight nearby counties, residents were braced for a "proactive power shutoff" that could extend for a day or more.

The morning of 8 November came, and the winds were barreling down the canyon, but the power was never shut off. At 7:56 a.m., more than an hour after the wildfire had begun, PG&E was still advising residents that it was considering the option of turning off the power "due to potential extreme fire danger." But the electricity stayed on until the blaze itself, growing by a football field every second, took it down.

Even as scores of people were being burned alive and thousands more were frantically fleeing a ridge overstuffed with traffic, the utility decided to compose a tweet. It was sent out at 3:14 p.m. and informed residents not of the fire and its path but the reasons why PG&E had decided not to turn off the power. Four months later, in the dust of ashes, the tweet not only sounded cold-hearted but read like the first act in the utility's effort to cover its tracks. "PG&E has determined that it will not proceed with plans today for a Public Safety Power Shutoff in portions of 8 Northern CA counties, as weather conditions did not warrant this safety measure," the tweet stated. "We want to thank our customers for their understanding."

By the time I left the ridge in early March, PG&E was conceding that one of its aging metal towers, which stood 100 feet (thirty meters) tall in the canyon twenty-five miles (forty kilometers) beyond Paradise, was so decrepit that a live wire had broken free of its grasp on the early morning of 8 November. This was the spark that birthed the deadliest wildfire in California history. That the culprit was the nation's biggest utility—its service area stretching seventy thousand square miles (180,000 square kilometers) from Bakersfield to the Oregon border, with a hundred thousand miles

"Even as scores of people were being burned alive and thousands more were frantically fleeing a ridge overstuffed with traffic, the utility decided to compose a tweet. It was sent out at 3:14 p.m. and informed residents not of the fire and its path but the reasons why PG&E had decided not to turn off the power."

(160,000 kilometers) of distribution lines and sixteen million customers—meant that whatever punishment came to it would reverberate far and wide. It was no small corporate disgrace when the monopoly, whose grab reached back more than a century and scarcely knew comeuppance, filed for bankruptcy a few months after the fire. The utility now found itself in multiple courtrooms trying to stave off $30 billion in liabilities for the devastation of Paradise and a series of earlier catastrophic fires it had caused.

In 2015, court records showed, PG&E's equipment ignited 435 fires, including a blaze traced to a single spindly gray pine that the utility had failed to remove. The tree leaned over and touched a high-voltage power line, sparking a wildfire that burned across Calaveras County, scorching 70,868 acres (28,680 hectares), destroying 549 homes and killing two people. In 2016, the same year PG&E neglected to cut down between four thousand and six thousand trees identified as "hazards," the utility recorded 362 wildfires of varying sizes.

Then, in a single month in 2017, the utility's repeated failures to manage danger—risks common to freighting power across great swaths of rugged terrain to deliver light and gas—caused

death and destruction on a scale that had seemed unimaginable. On or around the night of 8 October, nearly a dozen fires broke out in Napa, Mendocino, Solano, Lake, Butte, Calaveras, Nevada, and Yuba counties. The flames kept raging until they killed twenty-two people, destroyed four thousand houses and businesses and consumed 200,000 acres (80,940 hectares). The so-called North Bay Fires would set a record for ravage that would hold for exactly eleven months.

Now PG&E's legal team, led by a $1,100-an-hour Manhattan attorney named Kevin Orsini, gathered in a US district courtroom in downtown San Francisco awaiting another rap on the knuckles from federal judge William Alsup. The 73-year-old Mississippian, who had gone to Harvard Law and clerked for Supreme Court Justice William O. Douglas before a career in private practice and the Justice Department led to the bench, was presiding over an unusual hearing. PG&E had been deemed a corporate felon for its role in the deaths of eight people who were killed in 2010 when a company gas line blew up a neighborhood in the Bay Area city of San Bruno. As part of its ongoing probation, PG&E vowed not to commit another federal, state, or local crime. What to deem the 109 additional dead bodies—victims of wildfires ignited

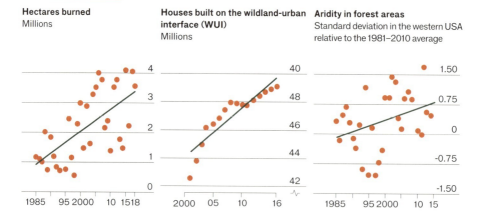

Hectares burned
Millions

Houses built on the wildland-urban interface (WUI)
Millions

Aridity in forest areas
Standard deviation in the western USA relative to the 1981–2010 average

SOURCE: THE ECONOMIST

by the utility over the past three years—if not evidence of more crimes?

"There is a very clear-cut pattern here: that PG&E is starting these fires," Judge Alsup said. "The drought did not start the fire. Global warming did not start the fire. PG&E started it. What do we do? Does the judge just turn a blind eye and say, 'PG&E, continue your business as usual. Kill more people by starting more fires?'"

"We have an inherently dangerous product is the fact," conceded Orsini, a partner at Cravath, Swaine & Moore, one of the nation's top law firms. "We have electricity running through high-power lines in areas that are incredibly susceptible to wildfire conditions."

"Do you know how much of California burned down last year?" Alsup asked. "1.6 per cent burned down last year. 1.6 per cent. The year before it was 1.3 per cent. That's almost 3 per cent of the acreage of the entire state burned up in two years. This is an emergency."

"PG&E understands and accepts that it has a credibility problem," Orsini replied, "which is why I couldn't stand up here and say to Your Honor, 'Trust us. We've got it.'"

A handful of litigators from three hard-charging Northern California law firms were representing close to a thousand survivors who had lost family members or houses or both in the 2017 and 2018 wildfires. They were pursuing their lawsuits not in Alsup's federal courtroom but in state court. In their filings, each attorney traced the historic blazes to a culture of mismanagement, corruption, and cover-up that had taken hold inside PG&E decades before. A pattern of venality, they argued, began in the company's early years and became more recalcitrant in the 1980s and 1990s when PG&E, with the connivance of the California Public Utilities Commission, its appointed watchdog, made a decision to place profits and bonuses to top executives—and dividends to shareholders—over safety.

"When you connect the dots, you see a culture of arrogance in which the most important thing is the bottom line," Frank Pitre, an attorney representing dozens of victims, told me. "Time and again, PG&E delays the necessary fixes, callously disregards the safety of California communities, and finds creative ways to not comply with law. Billions of dollars that should have been invested in infrastructure instead went to pay an 8 per cent return to its investors. That is their gold standard." It was fiction that the California Public Utilities Commission exercised any watchdog role over PG&E, he said. "They don't have the resources, they don't have the trained personnel or mindset, to monitor and audit PG&E's compliance with safety regulations. PG&E can literally get away with murder."

Judge Alsup ruled that the utility had violated the terms of a probation imposed after being convicted of six crimes in the San Bruno case. He then ordered its directors and top executives to board a bus and ride the Skyway and glimpse the gutting of Paradise, if not as an act of contrition than at least to remind themselves of their duties before the new fire season arrived. "The emergency will be on us, and will we see another headline, 'PG&E has done it again, they've burned down another town'?" he asked.

Yet for all his tough talk, he refrained from imposing any further conditions on PG&E to help protect the public from potential crimes in the future. To prod Alsup, plaintiffs' attorneys filed hundreds of pages of complaints, declarations, and memoranda of points that echoed the same theme: PG&E's refusal to heed the lessons of a series of destructive wildfires led to the burning down of Paradise.

Between 2014 and 2017, PG&E had sparked 1,552 wildfires, nine of them greater than 300 acres (120 hectares). Because PG&E took in a big swath of California that contained millions of dead and dying trees, the utility insisted that it was burdened with a perilous mission. If that was the case, attorneys for the plaintiffs countered, it was even more unconscionable that PG&E had waited so long to adopt measures to prevent wildfires and save lives—fixes that the state's other two major utilities had already implemented. These included installing state-of-the-art wind measuring stations, shutting off power during high-risk periods, replacing wooden poles with metal poles, dispatching teams of trained arborists to clear out trees too close to high-voltage lines.

"In the last five years, $4.5 billion of dividends have been paid out to the owners of PG&E," Judge Alsup said. "Some of the money could have been used to cut and trim the very trees that started these fires. So why is it PG&E says all the time, 'Safety is our number-one thing'? 'Safety. Safety. Safety.' But safety is not your number-one thing."

Judge Alsup then addressed the choice that faced PG&E on the early morning of 8 November 2018: to shut off the power and create a safety risk for a small number of residents—those on ventilators, those whose cell phones had died, those who couldn't open their garage doors to drive their vehicles—or not to shut off the power and possibly cause a spark that could light a wildfire that could kill scores of people?

"De-energizing is a safety risk," Orsini countered. "It's just a fact. How do we balance the safety risk of someone not being able to get the phone call telling them to flee a wildfire versus stopping a

"It was meant to be, we told ourselves. How else to explain that the smallest, most errant act did not arrive late, or at all, to fate's catenation? But it wasn't destiny that burned down Paradise."

wildfire that kills eighty-five people? How do you balance that?"

"Well, yes," Alsup replied, "but if the fire burns up the system anyway, then they're going to lose the power anyhow. Maybe it was the right judgment. I don't know. I don't know. But if that power had been turned off, that fire wouldn't have started, at least [not in] the same way."

It was the closest the courtroom would come to the question of the tragedy's construction, how circumstances large and small over decades—acts of arrogance and greed, blunder and corruption, neglect and design—could fasten upon each other and link up with acts of nature in perfect continuity and turn a company's risk into a community's erasure. Because the events that disordered our lives relied on such a diabolical ordering, it made us believe in the possibility of destiny. *It was meant to be*, we told ourselves. How else to explain that the smallest, most errant act did not arrive late, or at all, to fate's catenation? But it wasn't destiny that burned down Paradise.

On this day, no such pronouncements came down from the bench. In a federal courtroom not two miles from the headquarters of PG&E, the judge's equivocation would be the last word.

*

It was day, and it was night. Kathy Peppas was running down the Skyway, clutching the hand of her seven-year-old granddaughter Khloe as the smoke went from gray to black. Embers and pinecones, the oil inside sizzling, whizzed past their heads. Like little arsonists, they were taking the fire to the next ground, and the next ground. Peppas, fifty-four years old and fit, could hear the bullets shooting off from all the private stockpiles of ammo and guns in Paradise. Tanks of propane across the ridge were blowing up, too. "Count the explosions," she instructed Khloe, thinking it might take her granddaughter's mind off the flames. The girl counted to forty-five explosions, uttered close to a dozen prayers, and then told her grandmother that she had to pee. "Pee on yourself, honey," she told her. "It's all right."

Both sides of the Skyway were clogged with cars headed in the same direction: down the hill, and, if they were lucky, out into the open toward Chico. Others, like Peppas, had abandoned their cars and were now running for their lives. A lone fire engine rode up the ridge, the firefighters shouting at motorists to pull over to the side so they could get by. Frustrated, the men in blue decided to unleash their hoses right there. They shot a piss stream of water into a forest of burning trees. The absurdity almost made Peppas laugh. Her house, the houses belonging to her son, her mother, her sister and brother, her in-laws and nephews and niece, a dozen family houses in all, were going up in flames. So was the Church of the Latter-day Saints where she'd worshipped since she was Khloe's

In the late summer of 2020 in Napa Valley, North America's most important wine region, one of the most devastating fires in Californian history broke out. The flames even spread among the vines, which had always acted as a barrier: 363,220 hectares of land were burned, and six people lost their lives. Wildfires breaking out in the valley are nothing new: Native Americans constantly lit them, but they relied on a very different ecosystem, one that has now almost vanished. For thousands of years the land was dotted with oaks (whose wood does not burn easily) and needed fire to return to fertility, while the smoke cleaned the crowns of the trees, lowering the temperature on the ground. But the oaks were felled to increase sunlight exposure, which the vines need, and the pesticides and fertilisers used by many wine growers led to excessive vegetation growth, which is no longer burned off. Local farmers will therefore have to deal with the consequences of the fires in the longer term. There is still no detailed understanding of the effects of smoke on the vines, but exposure of the fruit can certainly have damaging results for the wine, which means less valuable harvests that end up being sold at a discount. One solution promoted by some wine growers would be to carry out controlled burns, but this is opposed by the body that monitors local air quality. Other solutions rely on higher-tech farming methods, but after the trauma of 2020, to many producers it seems to make more sense to lower their expectations in light of a changing climate and a compromised ecosystem.

age. But she and her granddaughter and the rest of the family came out alive.

Peppas and her husband Tom, a fly-fishing guide, bought a trailer and parked it at a house in Chico that belonged to friends. They always had planned on spending the rest of their lives in Paradise, but it was going to take a year at least for the ash and other contaminants to be removed and clean water to be restored and the lots cleared for rebuilding. Most of the evacuees she encountered in Chico were sure of one thing: they weren't coming back. There was too much uncertainty, they told her, and that didn't count the next wildfire. The local chamber of commerce, building trades, churches, and civic clubs were trying mightily to persuade them otherwise. Each week day, as Peppas drove up the ridge to her office job at a school untouched by the fire, she read the signs planted along the Skyway: "Rebuild. Recoup. Recover." "The Best Is Yet to Come." "Don't Stop Believing." "We Are Ridge Strong."

Then one by one, her four sons, who ranged in age from twenty-four to thirty-two, reached out to tell her what Paradise had meant to them. Three of them were living elsewhere and were now planning to move back home. There would be more grandchildren to tend to. "Right after the fire, I thought for a few minutes that we should live somewhere else," Peppas said. "But where would that be? I don't know how to live anywhere else. All the people close to me are Paradise people. And now the rest of my family was coming back. You have to understand what life here was all about. When my son Kevin got married a few years before the fire, we had the wedding reception at the church, and the food, the music, the decorations, all of it, was handled by friends

THE PASSENGER   Mark Arax

Pages 146–7: An aerial photograph of a Paradise neighbourhood wiped out in the fire.

and family. They built a dancefloor right there on the parking lot. From seven in the morning to eleven at night, they didn't stop working. How do you find that somewhere else?"

The town was debating how it should rise again. Council sessions were consumed with questions of existence. How big should a reborn Paradise be? Would a sewer system at last be dug? Would mobile homes by the hundreds be allowed back in? Or would the town be a place mostly for affluent retirees and middle-class workers who had jobs down the hill and could afford the more expensive real estate? In June 2019, PG&E settled with the county of Butte and the town of Paradise for $1 billion. How much infrastructure and civic building would that money buy? Could a new Paradise be made safer from wildfire? Governor Gavin Newsom, in a departure from Governor Jerry Brown, was calling out PG&E and pledging to reform the public utilities commission. Cal Fire, whose new director and his predecessor had backgrounds

THE PASSENGER   Mark Arax

Since the devastating San Francisco earthquake of 1906 – and thanks, too, to Hollywood – the San Andreas Fault, which marks the tectonic divide between the North American Plate and the Pacific Plate, is probably the world's most famous geological feature and the most forensically studied. For years California has been waiting for "the big one", an earthquake that will (probably) hit Southern California. Less well known is the risk (actually, the near certainty, even though no one is sure when) of a much more devastating earthquake – "the *really* big one" – somewhere on the (less iconic) Cascadia Subduction Zone, which follows the Pacific coast more or less from Vancouver Island in Canada to Mendocino in Northern California. As the journalist Kathryn Schulz explained in an article for *The New Yorker* (which won her the Pulitzer Prize in 2016), in spite of a long history of volcanic activity, there was no reason to think that the area was a seismic risk until scholars in the 1980s reconstructed a mega-earthquake that occurred in 1700 by putting together various clues, from an "orphan" tsunami recorded in Japan to the "ghost forest" of Oregon (where the coast had sunk, submerging the trees in the briny mud) and the oral traditions of Indigenous people. Following that discovery, it has been calculated that in the past ten thousand years there have been forty-one earthquakes with an average frequency of one every 241 years – so we are more than eighty years overdue. Above all, unlike most of California, which is aware of being built on a fault line, the Pacific Northwest is in no way prepared to face the *really* big one.

in forest management, was hiring more on-the-ground crews and spending more resources to clear out brush and trim trees. Would the ancient practice of controlled burns return as a force?

Peppas believed that she and the other survivors owed it to the eighty-five dead to fashion a considerably smaller Paradise that was better designed to handle wildfire's peril. She understood that the danger could never be fully taken out of the ridge and that climate change would make life here more of a gamble. Residents would need to pay higher fees to local government and higher premiums to insurers to help cover the risk. The new houses would likely be built with metal roofs and sprinkler systems. Roads would be paved where none existed before. Already, thousands of ponderosa pines and cedars had been removed. Half the trees that used to shade their old lot were gone. "It takes a while to get used to the light," she said.

I said goodbye to her on the ridge and drove back down into the valley, past the charred forest and the green line of Chico and the old orchards and dairy farms. The year had been a wet one. As I skirted the delta supercharged with snowmelt, I imagined the midsummer of 1839 when John Sutter, fugitive from Switzerland, father of the California myth, got lost in the tule swamps looking for the mouth of the Sacramento River. When he finally found it, he thought nothing of locating his New Helvetia, the future state capitol, in the embrace of not one river but two, the worst floodplain in all of California. The city of Sacramento, girdled by levees and erected on a twelve-foot (3.5-meter) bed of borrowed earth, its gilded state-house stabbing at sun, could not have looked more fitting and imperiled 180 years later. 🐦

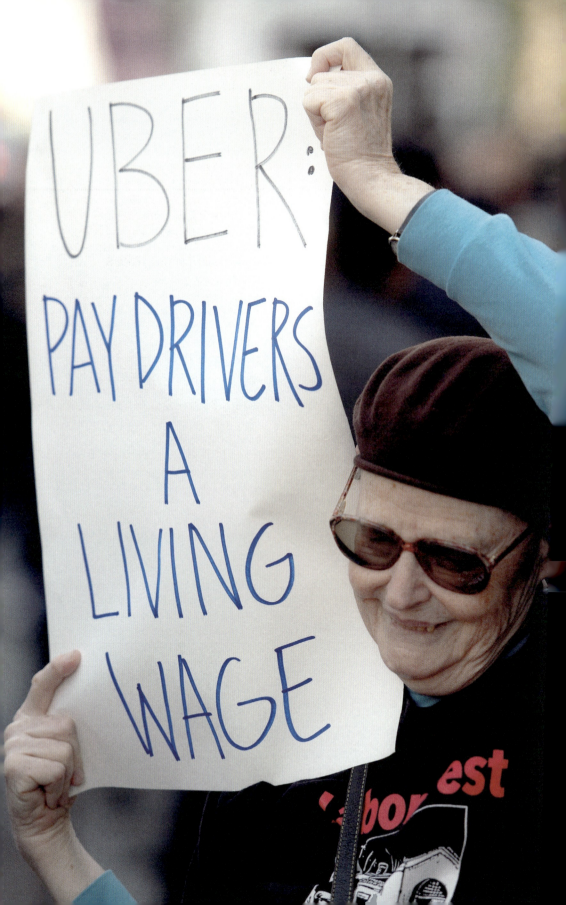

Ballot-Box Blues: The Indirect Road to Direct Democracy

Direct democracy in California takes many forms, sometimes unexpected, and the results of the various ballot initiatives are not always foregone conclusions. Here we take a look at this essential democratic tool through two of the most controversial propositions of recent times.

NC HERNANDEZ
Photographs by Josh Edelson and Jana Ašenbrennerová

Protests against Uber and Lyft at Uber's headquarters in San Francisco.

I had begun to notice cars with giant fuzzy pink mustaches attached to their front-sides since the time of the San Francisco Pride parade in June, so I thought they were holdover revelers from the city's vibrant gay scene traversing the gridded streets of the Golden City. I had cleared my morning schedule that day so I could cast a ballot, still preferring in-person voting to voting by mail. I was among the three-quarters of California's registered voters to cast a ballot by the end of the day. The polling station was only a block from my Mission District building—I saw two of the pink-mustachioed vehicles on that short walk—located in the rec room of an apartment complex for seniors. The makeshift nature, slovenly dressed poll watchers, and confused poll workers crossing names off paper lists, belied the gravity of a presidential election, but most polling stations in San Francisco are set up in unused common areas of apartment buildings or in someone's garage with the door propped open. Miraculously, the error rate remains below 3 per cent. Obama was sliding into an easy second-term victory, and our local senator, Dianne Feinstein, also had another uneventful win. Those votes felt perfunctory, like playing a role in the theater of electoral politics. It was the state ballot initiatives, spawned by the types of direct democracy that exist in twenty-four states, that would grate against the image of California as an easy-going liberal state. Proposition 34 intended to repeal the death penalty in the state, and it was endorsed by the unlikely cross-section of families of victims, the families of the wrongfully convicted, and law enforcement officials. Proposition 37 intended to force food suppliers to label genetically modified food. Both propositions began as signature-gathering measures. Both seemed to embody the liberal ideals of the West Coast. Both propositions failed.

For over a hundred years, California has had a ballot initiative system built on direct democracy. Begun during the early 20th century, the system has evolved through the years but has maintained the same intent: to allow a mechanism for individual citizens to organize their fellow Californians and force changes in law, constitution, or leadership. In its simplest form, it works like this: a citizen or group of citizens can make a single-subject proposal in writing, accompanied by a $2,000 filing fee, to the

NC HERNANDEZ is a Chicano writer from Southern California who lives in Mexico City with his wife and two cats. He has worked as a behaviourist for children with autism, a touring musician and an immigrants'-rights activist who led the first visiting programme in California for federally imprisoned immigrants. Hernandez writes sociopolitical essays about male violence, music and classic menswear.

> **"Two recent propositions help illuminate the political orbit of California ... reminding idealizers that if California were a liberal bastion by the sea, its fortifications stopped fifty miles inland, leaving two hundred miles up to interpretation."**

state's attorney general, who will title it, summarize it in one hundred words or fewer, and put it up for public comment for thirty days. If the authors survive the thirty days, their hardest task is ahead of them as they attempt to gather enough signatures to make the ballot. Taking vote tallies from the most recent gubernatorial election in the state, proponents have 180 days to gather 5 per cent for statutes or 8 per cent for constitutional amendments. If a proponent can accomplish their task, the signatures are turned in for verification to their respective county election officials. If the signatures are valid, the proposition is placed on the ballot for a vote. It's a system at times chaotic, at times empowering, and at times absurd.

Critiques of the ballot initiative system often include commentary on its exclusivity, citing not only the $2,000 filing fee—an $1,800 increase passed in 2015 to counter frivolous initiatives after someone filed a proposal to kill sodomites and another person filed a response proposal to force bigots into sensitivity training—but also the prohibitive costs of collecting signatures in California's fifty-eight counties. Even with large volunteer support, the cost-per-required-signature is several dollars, costing proponents millions just to get on the ballot. This type of direct democracy, its detractors say, is arguably neither democratic nor direct.

GRASS ROOTS

Two recent propositions help illuminate the political orbit of California. Props 64

and 22 each offered different versions of success and reminded idealizers that if California were a liberal bastion by the sea, its fortifications stopped fifty miles (eighty kilometers) inland, leaving two hundred miles up to interpretation; a mix of Wild West leftovers and rural conservatism. But these propositions proved to be far more complex in their making. From these stories emerged Jason Calacanis and Dennis Peron, respectively embodying the venture capitalists that ran through California like packs of dogs (we'll call them *Cali canis major*) and the grassroots hippies that pushed to *legalize it* (we'll call them *Cali cannabis minor*).

Prop 64, also known as the Adult Use of Marijuana Act (AUMA), built on existing legislation that allowed for the legal use of marijuana for medical purposes and expanded it to allow for recreational use for adults over the age of twenty-one. To understand the story of AUMA, we need to go back to the early 1970s and the burgeoning gay-rights movement in San Francisco's Castro District to look at Peron's formative years in marijuana advocacy. As was a common trajectory at the time, he passed through the ranks of the air force and 1968's Tet Offensive and finally landed in San Francisco, where he turned on and became a Yippie. The Youth International Party was known for anarchist politics and political theatre that satirized authority, and Peron began to organize smoke-ins, where large gatherings of people would smoke marijuana openly and in defiance of the law. He

Above: Friends Emily Gilmore and Shannon Washburn smoke a joint at the 420 Hippie Hill celebrations in San Francisco's Golden Gate Park. **Opposite:** Cannabis on sale at a marijuana dispensary in San Francisco.

(IL)LEGALISE IT

In 2016 legalisation of recreational cannabis use in California was approved by 60 per cent of voters in the hope of creating a flourishing market and replenishing state coffers with the resulting tax receipts – and yet 89 per cent of the market remains illegal today, primarily because of the difficulties in covering the costs of legalisation. Tax pressure is high, regulations extensive and distribution is complex because municipalities can make up their own minds as to whether to comply or not with legalisation (and many do not). It is significant that in an area of widespread cannabis cultivation like Humboldt County, the majority opposed legalisation in 2016. This was partly for historical reasons – home to hippie communities in the 1960s, the county has retained some of its original opposition to "the man"

– but more than that it was because the growers, with an entrepreneurial mindset, had enjoyed huge profits and no regulation for some twenty years since medical marijuana became legal in 1996, leading to growing demand but no corresponding increase in checks or taxes. Now it is difficult for these growers to find space in the market except with niche, high-quality products, so the alternative is the black market, which, paradoxically, legalisation has favoured, because prosecuting those who sell and grow marijuana is no longer a priority for the police. But the illegal market brings with it serious and large-scale consequences: those who work in it have no legal protection, water resources are indiscriminately exploited and illegal pesticides poison the land and the water table – and, running alongside this, turf disputes are gradually growing bloodier.

soon began selling marijuana out of a storefront, enduring multiple raids by the cops, and supporting Harvey Milk, the first openly gay elected official in the state. Peron's attention quickly shifted from political mockery to medicinal marijuana advocacy when the Aids epidemic struck the gay community. By the 1990s, he was considered the godfather of the marijuana legalization movement and began to focus on using the ballot initiative system to write legislation, finally attaining citywide medical-use permission in 1991 and opening the country's first legal-marijuana dispensary before achieving statewide medical-use permission five years later.

This was how far the grassroots movement was able to go in California, and, despite large public-opinion campaigns to sway the minds of the voters,

recreational legalization was still twenty years off. Proposition 19, known as the Regulate, Control, and Tax Cannabis Act, was narrowly defeated in 2010 with only 47 per cent of the vote. Six years later, AUMA was on the ballot and passed with 57 per cent of the vote. What changed in these six years that flipped the numbers so drastically? Of course, there were the test cases of marijuana legalization in Colorado and Washington followed by Oregon and Alaska, which softened the stodgy opposition in California across most demographic groups, but many of the older folks were still clearly embroiled in the remnants of "Reefer Madness" fear mongering—Senator Dianne Feinstein made the claim that primetime television was going to be advertising marijuana, a claim that was quickly debunked as false. A 2015 Pew Research Center poll stated

Direct democracy is a full-time job

A far from exhaustive list of referendums
held over the past twenty years

PROPOSITION 66 (2004)

A proposed amendment to the so-called "Three-Strikes" law for repeat offenders, which stipulates a 25-year sentence for the third serious offence. The proposition would have required the third offence to be particularly violent and/or serious for the sentence to be imposed and would have altered the definition of certain offences. A campaign led by the governor at the time, Arnold Schwarzenegger, on the risk of releasing "26,000 dangerous criminals and rapists" turned the polls around at the last minute.

NO

52.7%

PROPOSITION 69 (2004)

The "DNA Initiative" allowed the collection of DNA samples from those arrested for certain crimes. California currently maintains the world's third largest DNA database.

YES

62%

"That marijuana became a pet project of the rich played no small part in its acceptance by the power structures in the state."

that, after legalization in these other states, attitudes about recreational marijuana were essentially the same around the entire country, not just in California. In a rare alignment of political attitudes between the reddest states and the blue beacon of the West, the US mellowed on the weed issue.

But it was the major funding that also set this proposition apart, costing the campaign around $25 million before making the ballot. One contributor alone spent nearly $9 million. That this became a pet project of the rich played no small part in its acceptance by the power structures in the state. That generous contributor was a venture capitalist in San Francisco, one of the founders of the file-sharing application Napster and part of the moneyed right-wing libertarian tech crowd that cozies up to whichever political party is most expedient. The liberal political system of California has long sided with big business; it is no coincidence that California has the largest economy in the country. These rising stars of venture capitalism were not among the *Cali cannabis minor* seeking compassionate access to marijuana rights, but they were willing to

---

PROPOSITION 71 (2004)

The law on "Stem-Cell Research and Cures" represents a unique case of electors deciding to fund scientific research directly (a role generally played by the federal government), not only making stem-cell research a constitutional right but authorising bond issues to raise $3 billion over ten years for research and research facilities.

YES

59%

PROPOSITION 73 (2005)

The "Parental Notification of Abortion Initiative" would have made it compulsory to inform the parents of a minor intending to have an abortion forty-eight hours in advance (except in the event of a medical emergency).

NO

52.8%

PROPOSITION 8 (2008)

Known as "Prop 8" or "the Mormon Proposition", it called for the abolition of same-sex marriage rights (introduced by a ruling from the Supreme Court of California a few months earlier). Following a heated legal battle, Prop 8 was declared unconstitutional in 2013.

YES

52.2%

---

align themselves with this cause, keeping in mind the long-term profitability of the legal-marijuana market.

MONEY MOVES

In 2020, Prop 22—also going under the title Exempts App-Based Transportation and Delivery Companies from Providing Employee Benefits to Certain Drivers Initiative Statute (the Yes on Prop 22 campaign claimed in a lawsuit that the title was biased, but the court did not agree)—was a groundbreaking proposition, not in that it was written by the corporate sector to subvert state law but because, with over $200 million in funding, it was the most expensive ballot proposal in California history. Prop 22 created a nebulous third class for gig-economy workers between independent contractor and employee,

providing some additional benefits that independent contractors don't have but falling far short of the full protection enjoyed by employees. This new third class of employment classification was obfuscated with tech-hipster jargon about entrepreneurship, partnership, and freedom, but in the end they were using the ballot initiative system as a reach past government to design their own employment laws.

To understand the story of Prop 22 we need to go back to 2018 and look at the California Assembly Bill 5 (AB5). AB5 was a state statute meant to codify a recent state supreme court decision that laid out clear delineations between an independent contractor and an employee. An independent contractor must control their own labor and time, engage in similar work on a regular basis, and be

PROPOSITION 28 (2012)	
A constitutional amendment to change the state's legislative-term limits from eight years for the Senate and six for the Assembly to twelve for both houses. A similar proposition had failed in 2008.	YES 61%
PROPOSITION 47 (2014)	
With the aim of reducing the prison population, this proposition would have reclassified certain non-violent offences – including shoplifting, theft, fraud (up to the value of $950), possession of drugs for personal use – as misdemeanours rather than felonies. The money saved by the state would have been spent on school-drop-out prevention, mental health and drug-misuse treatment.	NO 59.6%
PROPOSITION 56 (2016)	
After two failed attempts in 2006 and 2012 this proposition increased tax on cigarettes to $2 a pack, with most of the new revenues destined for Medi-Cal, the state health programme for those on low incomes.	YES 64.4%

providing a service outside the scope of the business they are contracting with. Gig-economy businesses such as Uber and Lyft lobbied to have their companies placed on the exemptions list but were denied. They weren't alone in their disapproval; musicians and truck drivers also often fell between the cracks of typical employment classification, and they, too, sought special consideration lest their professions be adversely affected. But once refused inclusion in the exemption list, Uber and Lyft took a different stance altogether; they chose to disregard AB5 in its entirety and refused to reclassify gig workers as employees. In turn, the California attorney general sued the rideshare companies, and in the summer of 2020 the court ruled against Uber and Lyft and said that they were misclassifying gig workers as independent contractors. On 10 August 2020, the companies were given ten days to comply with AB5, but they threatened to shut down their rideshare services across the state. Through the app, users were sent an ominous message declaring services to be terminated across California on 20 August. On that date, the companies announced they were granted an extension by the court until 4 November. They wasted no time in crafting the language of Prop 22 so it could reach the ballot by 3 November.

The rideshare companies constructed something that at first glance appears to be a kind of middle ground but under closer scrutiny appears to lean far to the right. Prop 22 provides a healthcare stipend that accrues with hours worked but stops short of providing health insurance. There is no job security

---

PROPOSITION 60 (2016)

Modelled on a measure approved by referendum in Los Angeles County in 2012, Proposition 60 would have made the use of condoms compulsory in porn films, as well as appropriate vaccinations and medical examinations for the performers at the producers' expense. The porn industry employs around two thousand people in California and is estimated to be worth $9 billion.

NO

53.7%

PROPOSITION 67 (2016)

A proposition banning single-use plastic or paper bags but permitting the sale of recycled, reusable paper bags. A related measure, Proposition 65, to allocate the revenues generated by the sale of disposable bags to the Wildlife Conservation Fund, was defeated by 53.9 per cent of the votes.

YES

53.3%

PROPOSITION 9 (2018)

The "Cal 3 Initiative" launched by the venture capitalist Tim Draper called for California to be divided into three separate states. The proposition was withdrawn before the vote by the Supreme Court of California, which subsequently removed such a measure definitively from all future ballots.

WITHDRAWN

when demand is low, but the companies boast that workers have the freedom to choose their own schedules. It provides for 120 per cent of the minimum wage but only pays for what it calls "engaged time," meaning drivers are only paid for the time they have a rider in their car but not for time between rides, drastically reducing the per-hour wage. Some estimates have brought this to below six dollars an hour when demand is low, less than half of any California minimum wage. What the proposition doesn't provide is sick leave, overtime compensation, unemployment insurance, sexual harassment or discrimination protections, or the collective-bargaining rights that employees enjoy, but it also forces gig-economy workers to forego the small-business controls of independent contractors, such as cultivating their own client base or setting their own prices. It really is the worst of both worlds. Another novel aspect of Prop 22 is a small proviso that states that it would require seven-eighths of the legislature to agree to make any amendments, rather than the typical two-thirds needed, effectively quashing any legislative resistance to the measure. It would seem that the only challenge left that could overturn it would be another ballot measure. It is worth noting here that Uber has yet to turn a profit, although their net loss shrank in 2021 to around $100 million, so profitability may prove to be around the corner after all, now that rideshare services have become ubiquitous in California.

Uber, in collaboration with DoorDash, Lyft, Instacart, and Postmates, poured money and resources into backing Prop 22. These companies either pressured

PROPOSITION 10 (2018) This proposition sought to expand the authority of local governments to impose limits on residential rents (repealing the 1995 Costa-Hawkins Act) but was rejected following electors' fears of an increase in bureaucracy and regulations on single-family homes.	 **59.4%**
PROPOSITION 12 (2018) The "Farm Animal Confinement Initiative" sets out new minimum requirements for farmers to provide more space for laying hens, breeding pigs and veal calves. The law strengthened measures already approved in 2008's Proposition 2.	 **62.6%**
PROPOSITION 16 (2020) Proposition 16 sought to repeal 1996's Proposition 209, which prohibited the use of affirmative action, or positive discrimination, in the public sector. The ban on government institutions taking race, sex or ethnicity into account in public employment remains in force, although socioeconomic considerations are permitted.	 **57.2%**

management overtly to promote the Yes on 22 campaign to employees or else forced workers to include Yes on 22 stickers with every customer's order, printed grocery bags with Yes on 22 emblazoned on the side, and developed a pop-up window within their apps that gave drivers the option with every ride to "Support 22" or click "OK." The latter choice would cause the pop-up to return with the same question on the next ride until attrition led many drivers to click the former, driving up numbers in the companies' "Gig-Economy Workers Support Prop 22" data. Ads were on constant rotation on television and radio, in print and public spaces, with language like "Prop 22 will provide guaranteed earnings and a healthcare stipend" and "Prop 22 is Progress." The Yes on Prop 22 campaign was effective despite the

litany of progressive and liberal names endorsing the No on Prop 22 campaign, including Joe Biden, Bernie Sanders, Elizabeth Warren, Kamala Harris, Alexandria Ocasio-Cortez, and former US secretary of labor Robert Reich. The Yes on Prop 22 campaign outspent its opponents by more than ten to one, and the investment paid off on election day when it passed with 59 per cent of the vote.

Where Uber largely flew under the radar in its early days, discreetly picking up passengers in private cars, Lyft drivers announced themselves with an oversized fuzzy pink mustache affixed to the front of their cars that seemed to mock cabbies as they swooped in to collect fares for themselves. California taxi drivers began to complain to government officials about the rise of rideshare apps that were, as they saw it, stealing their business

PROPOSITION 24 (2020)

This proposition expanded the law on consumer privacy already approved by the legislature in 2018, giving people more control over their personal data and limiting businesses' use of "sensitive personal information", such as precise geolocation, race, ethnicity, religion, sexual orientation and health data.

56.2%

PROPOSITION NUMBERING

Originally, the numbers assigned to propositions were reset at each election, but this created potential confusion through the repetition of propositions with the same number from one year to another. In 1982 they began to be numbered in order, year after year, so that by 1996 people were voting for Proposition 200 and above. In 1998 the numbering was restarted and is now reset every ten years.

SOME FIGURES

Between 1910 and 2020 Californians have voted on 1,284 propositions. The 1970s was the decade with the most propositions (including the infamous Proposition 13 of 1978 on limiting property taxes), whereas the 1950s was the decade with the fewest. The record year for propositions was 1914, with forty-eight. California's constitution, which is ten times as long as its federal counterpart, has been amended some five hundred times since it was written in 1879, including forty changes following popular initiatives.

> "The political spectrum in the United States can appear skewed to outside observers. To the rest of the world, our liberals range from centrists to right-of-center, and the conservatives from right-of-center to far-right."

right out from under their noses while claiming to be innovating the industry. The supposed innovation was pure marketing, contended the taxi drivers as they pointed to their own app, Cabulous, which pre-dated both Uber and Lyft by two years. The real innovation may have been embedded in this new employment classification system that evaded government regulation rather than in the business model itself. Time will tell.

Currently, Prop 22 is tied up in litigation and appeals. In August 2021, a county court ruled the proposition to be unconstitutional and unenforceable, citing as one of the two reasons that the seven-eighths requirement to amend it stopped the legislature from being able to set standards for the workplace. The other violation, according to the court, was that Prop 22 was too expansive in its scope and therefore violated the single-subject rule of the California constitution, which states: "An initiative measure embracing more than one subject may not be submitted to the elector or have any effect." In the end, Prop 22 may have had eyes bigger than its stomach.

THE NAME YOU CAN'T RECALL

It is here that we return to the *Cali canis major*, the venture capitalists with visions of a libertarian utopia. "Have fun being poor," is a common line used in the venture-capitalist milieu to respond to pushback against what they see as the inevitability of corporate teleology. It is a phrase one hears in Jason Calacanis's

podcasts, where he discusses venture capitalism, angel investment, and startup businesses while warning about what he calls the "emerging hysterical socialist left." It seems to embody the *Innovate or Die* spirit in California tech that either aligns with or unwittingly emulates a libertarian business ideology that sees progress and deregulation as inevitable. Calacanis was an early investor in Uber, and as his fortune has grown he has solidified his position in California politics.

To understand the political positioning of the new-tech moneyed libertarians of California, some explanation is necessary. The political spectrum in the United States can appear skewed to outside observers. To the rest of the world, our liberals range from centrists to right-of-center, and the conservatives from right-of-center to far-right, though the general understanding within the US is that liberals are leftists, just to the right of Marxists, and that conservatives are moderates, just to the right of center. One need only compare the similarities of Germany's conservative Christian Democratic Union to the United States' liberal Democratic party to see how this ideological ambiguity makes political discussion outside the confines of our national borders difficult, but understanding this about United Statesians can help the reader to understand the following story.

When Chesa Boudin was elected San Francisco district attorney with only a sliver of a majority at the beginning of 2020, the right-wing propaganda, from both parties, came thundering down from the skies. In the 1970s, Boudin's parents were members of the far-left Weather Underground, whose militant use of political violence led to a domestic-terrorist designation by the FBI. When his parents participated in a 1981 armored-car heist, two police officers and a guard were shot dead. His parents were caught and sentenced to prison, despite never having fired a shot themselves. Boudin was adopted by one of the Weather Underground leaders, Bill Ayers, who later came to national attention in the 2008 presidential election as the University of Illinois at Chicago professor who had a supposed connection to Barack Obama. Boudin spent his childhood maintaining close relationships with his parents and visiting them often in prison. All of these associations painted Boudin as a far-left radical himself, and when the right-wing political forces in California aligned against him, they weaponized his background as cheap propaganda. He did campaign on criminal-justice reform, and he publicly takes a restorative-justice approach to prosecution rather than a retributive one, so even the establishment liberal media never fails to assign blame to the DA's office every time a crime can be exploited as a spectacle, despite the overall decline in crime rates across the city. It is worse if the offender has prior convictions or arrests, which they usually do, because the narrative becomes that the DA "let them walk free to commit more crimes because he cares more about criminals than law-abiding citizens." The media tends to focus on the crimes that are up, like murder, but fails to mention that not only were the last few years record lows for murder but

THE WEATHER UNDERGROUND

Not to be confused with Weather Report, the great jazz-fusion outfit that emerged in the same period, the Weathermen (later renamed the Weather Underground) was a militant movement established in the wake of protests against the Vietnam War. The name was taken from a line in Bob Dylan's "Subterranean Homesick Blues": "You don't need a weatherman to know which way the wind blows." Established as an extremist fringe of existing student collectives, it engaged in urban-guerrilla actions as a means of fighting imperialism and supported the Black liberation movement. Unlike other terrorist organisations at the time, its use of violence was mainly symbolic, and most of its attacks on institutions and police stations were preceded by warnings to ensure there were no victims, as was the case with the bombs at the Pentagon and the Capitol, two of their most high-profile targets. One cult episode in the history of Californian counterculture relates to the Weathermen's involvement in LSD guru Timothy Leary's escape from a state prison. In early 1970 the group went underground, with cells scattered between Berkeley, Chicago, Detroit and New York, and various members found themselves on the FBI's top-ten-most-wanted list. After the end of the Vietnam War terrorism ended up being largely consigned to history in the US, only really re-entering the national consciousness after 9/11. Curiously, that very same day *The New York Times* published an interview with the organisation's former leader Bill Ayers, who stated that he had no regrets other than not having done enough.

Above and opposite: Protests against Uber and Lyft in San Francisco.

the overall national murder rate is rising commensurate to San Francisco, demonstrating that the problem is not unique to the city.

There were two recall efforts against Boudin. The first failed in the summer of 2021, but, at the time of writing, the second has just submitted signatures for verification and will be on the June 2022 ballot if verified. The process to initiate a recall is not unlike other ballot initiatives in general, but there are two types of California recalls, in particular: recalls of state officials and recalls of local officials. Like the ballot initiative system,

a California citizen can file to begin the process, in this case a notice-of-intent-to-recall along with a perfunctorily small number of at least sixty-five voter signatures for state recalls, but if recalling a local official, the requisite number of signatures is equal to the number of nomination signatures needed to run for the office being recalled plus ten. In Boudin's case, that number was 11,772 plus ten. This strikes a strange imbalance between state and local recalls, but such is our system. Reasons for recalls can vary and largely don't matter. It is the signatures that count. If a recall gathers

enough signatures to be on the ballot, replacement candidates can begin to run their campaigns before being placed on the ballot next to the question asking yes or no to the recall. Federally elected officials cannot be recalled with this system.

The failed Boudin recall effort was started by a failed Republican mayoral candidate. The second recall was organized by two Democratic activists who are using essentially the same talking points as the failed recall effort but dressed up as progressive politics. This charade is only possible because of the skewed understanding of political ideology in the state. This is where Calacanis comes back into focus. Calacanis has taken up the cause of this second recall and has started an online fundraiser to hire a full-time investigative journalist to cover the DA's office in a ham-fisted attempt to dig up dirt on Boudin. Calacanis and the other venture-capitalist techies, some with murky connections to violent right-wing groups like the Proud Boys, could have easily funded this position themselves but have chosen to create a publicity spectacle instead. What we see, similar to Prop 22, is money using its power to influence politics by effectively

"In these confused times, it may be that the government we have is the government we deserve. There is an irony that our ballot initiative system is becoming one of big business."

purchasing direct democracy, and, as the younger libertarian tech crowd enters the picture, political lines are obfuscated by hip lingo and progressive rhetoric.

All of this was happening against the backdrop of the gubernatorial recall effort against current governor Gavin Newsom. It was easily crushed by establishment liberals but not before costing the state over $275 million. Recalls in California are common, but, of the nearly 180 attempts since the system was adopted in 1913, only six have been successful. One of the six was the 2003 recall of Governor Gray Davis that gave us Arnold Schwarzenegger, facetiously referred to at the time as "the Governator."

WEDNESDAY 7 NOVEMBER 2012
I remember feeling simultaneously surprised and not surprised that Props 34 and 37 failed. It may be that the political landscape indeed fades from blue to red the farther inland one travels from the beach. No amount of pink mustaches can obscure the political divisions in California. Prop 37, intended to label genetically modified foods, seemed like an obvious choice in the health-conscious city centers, but the fear of rising food prices in the rural parts of the state stacked the ballot against the proposition. Prop 34, which failed with only 48 per cent of the vote statewide—despite gaining 70 per cent of the vote in San Francisco County—would have made California the sixteenth state at the time

to abolish the death penalty. Six other states have abolished it since then, but California still has not. I can't help but think that the state's overall attitude to crime, be it the death penalty or the Boudin critiques based in some vague "life sentence for any infraction" implication, is reflected in these choices.

In these confused times, it may be that the government we have is the government we deserve. There is an irony that our ballot initiative system is becoming one of big business; its roots are in the reforms of the early-20th century's progressive movement, and it was designed to be a counterweight to the corrupt political machinations of the 19th century. This pendulum of political attitudes has defined the state since, opinions swinging between liberal and conservative. A long view may imply a leftward tilt to the state's orbit, but recent events seem to indicate an about-face on the horizon.

There is currently a battle over the theoretical framework of this direct democracy system being fought at the ballot boxes and in the courts. Are we to use it as a tool to shape our own political systems or as a weapon to squash political opposition? If recent US politics has taught us anything about predictions, it is that we are an unpredictable bunch, but I will remind the reader that democracy is a messy business and one rooted just as often in dissensus as in consensus. If one spends enough time around

Recall elections are quite common around the world, although there are differences in practice. How they work might be set out in a country's constitution and therefore apply nationally, or they might apply only in certain jurisdictions (the cities of some German *Länder*, parts of Argentina, British Columbia in Canada); they can be applied to every democratically elected representative (from a civil servant to the president, as in Venezuela and Colombia) or only to specific roles (mayors in Saxony and the entire Latvian parliament – but not individual members). The function of recall, however, is always the same, and that is to ensure that elected representatives remain representative of the will of the people and do not betray their promises to the electorate. They offer citizens a means of controlling those for whom they have voted – provided that a minimum number of signatures are collected for the procedure to begin (in some cases, so many are required that success is almost impossible). That's the theory, at least. Political scientists have long wondered if recall is an effective instrument of direct democracy or whether it could be transformed into a weapon for political destabilisation. A gauge for understanding what is going on is to analyse what convinces any group of electors to initiate a recall procedure and endeavour to collect the required number of signatures to proceed; this also allows analysts to understand the makeup of any group. The clear risk, however, is that such a procedure could turn into a political stratagem to delegitimise a majority.

activists, one will inevitably hear it said that the larger political fight is already lost and that the federal monster is too big to face head on, but local politics is still where it's at. Activists know that the power to disrupt the political machine lies in the fissures, the cracks, the small spaces in between the oiled and engineered parts, and so focus is often shifted to local and state propositions and elections. It is common to find activists who know more about the inner workings of their county's Board of Supervisors than they do about the United States Senate. If the ballot initiative system is being co-opted by big business, it is also still one of the only tools that local organizers have to effect change, and in that it is indispensable.

Perhaps beneath the Botoxed, suntanned exteriors there is a touch of the cowboy ethos and westward expansionism of California's early days still wrestling with the progressive reforms and radical politics of the 20th century. After four decades in the state, I can say that all of my critiques are of the same deeply personal variety one makes of family; that is, they are my own, and if an outsider voiced the same critiques, I, too, would be liable to engage in an about-face and assume a defensive posture. California's democratic future may be written in the stars, but if there is going to be room for democracy to thrive, we will first have to come out of this political retrograde. 🐦

Some of Everything

Young dancers perform in the annual Kingdom Day Parade in Los Angeles; the parade is the largest event marking Martin Luther King Jr. Day in Southern California.

Despite the gentrification that has reduced the African-American population of central Los Angeles to historic lows – down from 20 per cent in the 1970s to 8 per cent today – arts and culture are thriving within the Black community, a response, in part, to the widespread anger following the murder of George Floyd.

LISA TEASLEY
Photographs by Ringo Chiu

169

At the height of 2020's worldwide human rights protests in response to George Floyd's ruthless murder—a tipping point of countless organized uprisings in response to the horrifically savage and brutal structural system of racism and slavery that has existed in the US since 1619—I was asked by the publication *GO Magazine* how people involved in culture should respond to this moment. I stated, "Uplift and change can be found in creative collaboration in the same way that effective transformative human rights protests require organization and community building. So, artists in this moment can take this momentum that has been created and be of service in the healing of the collective soul by combining their gifts." This is what has been happening, as it has always been happening within the Black community: working in blood, sweat, and tears to take care of the people.

Now that the average price of a home in Los Angeles is a million dollars, with rampant gentrification and more than 50 per cent of properties flipped by cash investors, it is easily said that LA is a city sold to the highest bidder. With the long-term egregious effects of the Airbnb boom added to the pandemic, it is not difficult to unpack the tragically huge numbers of homeless who come (and are sent) from far and wide across the country to refuge in the warmer climes of Los Angeles, making it a city hardly recognizable as that portrayed in *Pretty Woman* or *Once Upon a Time in Hollywood*.

A Black female artist friend, who was pushed out of her LA Koreatown neighborhood some twelve years ago when the building was sold, has been living in the far more affordable Berlin ever since; and she has become a resident with excellent healthcare, something few people anywhere in the US can claim. Still, despite some of these challenges felt the world over, along with very sound reasons to flee this particular city—especially for people of color—LA's Black creatives are thriving with communal thinking, advocacy, and collaborative projects. These collaborations are not made exclusively Black and are done with grateful acknowledgement to the Indigenous peoples of these lands, the Tongva, Tataviam, and Chumash, as well as to the city's Latinx heritage, dating back to well before the City of Angels was ruled by a Mexico newly independent from Spain.

Artist Lauren Halsey created the South Central Los Angeles community center Summaeverythang, when acting on her dream and intention of hosting art talks, workshops, and events, and began building at the beginning of 2020; but when the pandemic struck she shifted her focus to distributing weekly local organic produce boxes that would be free to the community. Summaeverythang has been delivering goods from Southern California farms and distributing some six hundred boxes a week to the Watts and South Central communities, all funded by Halsey's own art sales and outside donations. In addition, the center has a hot meal program in operation

LISA TEASLEY is an American writer and visual artist. Her first book, the story collection *Glow in the Dark* (2002), won the Gold Pen and Pacificus Foundation awards. Her second and third books, the novels *Dive* (2004) and *Heat Signature* (2006), both received critical acclaim. Teasley is the writer and presenter of the BBC television documentary *High School Prom* (2006) and is an editor at large for the *Los Angeles Review of Books*. She lives in Los Angeles.

RINGO CHIU is a Pulitzer Prize-winning photojournalist whose work has been published around the world and received numerous awards, including the National Press Photographers Association's Best of Photojournalism, Los Angeles Press Club's Southern California Photojournalist of the Year on several occasions and the Best Hong Kong News Photography three years running. Born in China and raised in Hong Kong, he lives in Los Angeles.

since early 2021, with an impressive team of Crenshaw-area-based chefs such as rapper/chef Hugh Augustine, Southern Creole caterer Shanita Castle, Caribbean chef and caterer Stuart Eubanks, personal vegan and raw chef Supreme Dow, as well as Tim Hollingsworth from downtown LA's Otium restaurant.

Food, the essential to living along with unpolluted air to breathe and clean water to drink, has always been the gathering place for community. I spent most every Sunday of my childhood and early teen years at my Panamanian grandmother's house in the Historic West Adams District, which was one of the many Los Angeles areas to experience white flight until becoming predominantly Black by the time my mother arrived from Panama in the 1950s. The area is now predominantly white, but not without Jamaican, Ethiopian, Soul Food, and barbecue restaurants, a few examples of rich traditions in Black diaspora eating. As LA is one of the ten most culturally diverse cities in the world, the restaurant experience here is naturally a multitude of choices honoring that diversity, even as they have been hit hard by the pandemic and the BIPOC communities even harder.

The three artist and activist founders of the Crenshaw Dairy Mart in Inglewood have a vision of abolition, liberation from structural racism and food apartheid, and the creation of complete self-sustenance. The center is a gallery and abolitionist healing organization created in 2018 and launched in 2020 by Black Lives Matter co-founder and artist Patrisse Cullors along with fellow artists/activists noé olivas and alexandre ali reza dorriz. The Geffen Contemporary at the Museum of Contemporary Art in downtown LA invited the artists to exhibit in the summer of 2021, and at the same time they were asked to do the WeRise event sponsored by the Los Angeles County Department of Mental Health. There they exhibited the abolitionist pod, consisting of a garden growing within a geodesic dome, a prototype for this liberation from structural racism and food apartheid and becoming self-sustaining.

One of Crenshaw Dairy Mart's neighbors and collaborators, Juice Wood, along with Vernon Yancy, approached the founders about sponsoring a community fridge, which is one of around eighteen such fridges in various neighborhoods across Los Angeles. Each fridge is hosted and managed by galvanized local citizens, donated to by anyone who cares to, and it is kept open for all those in need. Feeding the people, as well as being an example and education for how to feed oneself, is paramount, but just as important is finding the joy within. Making space and time for music and dancing has always been essential for the human spirit.

I have been taking care of myself by dancing ever since I was less than a year old, pulling myself up to hold on to the stereo cabinet and shaking my butt to the Beethoven my father was playing, since classical music was all we listened to in our house. I heard salsa, rumba, and merengue at my grandmother's, where in her living room I would dance all evening

THE PASSENGER   Lisa Teasley

THE 8 PER CENT

The recent history of Black Los Angeles is a story of steep relative demographic decline. From a high of almost 20 per cent in the 1970s, coinciding with the peak of so-called "white flight" from US city centres, the proportion of African Americans in the population now stands at around 8 per cent, the result of the arrival of waves of immigration from Central America in a phenomenon known as "ethnic succession". This figure of 8 per cent has taken on a symbolic value, celebrating what remains of the Black community whose history forms an integral part of Los Angeles, above all of South Central, where three-quarters of the city's Black population traditionally lived. In Black areas of the city people were corralled into overcrowded neighbourhoods by segregationist policies, which were explicit in the pre-war period but somewhat subtler later, from redlining to the construction of freeways in the middle of Black residential areas in the name of urban regeneration, even in middle-class areas like Sugar Hill, which was cut in two by a freeway in 1963. Later, the decline of the industrial base of the city in the 1980s along with demographic changes brought unemployment, poverty and crack dealing, leading to "Black flight" from the widespread violence. Conversely, since the 2010s, with the gradual decline in crime, there has even been a "white return", the (re)gentrification of neighbourhoods in South Central (renamed South Los Angeles, partly to dissociate it from the stigma of violence), which makes the 8 per cent figure all the more emblematic: the Black community, even though it now represents a small minority of the total population of Los Angeles, still accounts for 34 per cent of its homeless population and 30 per cent of its prison inmates.

Page 172: The Festival of Masks at the eighth annual Day of the Ancestors in Leimert Park, Los Angeles. The festival includes a procession and live performances in which traditional artists, youth groups and various members of the community celebrate the global African village, paying tribute to a shared heritage.

Page 173: A demonstration in downtown Los Angeles on 5 June 2020 following the death of George Floyd, who was killed on 25 May while being arrested by the Minneapolis police.

with my many cousins. Then I heard funk, house, and hip hop at school and classmates' parties, which grew my taste into some of everything in the world that I could dance to. I would be hard pressed to find a genre of music that I cannot listen to, as long as it is good. So I greatly appreciate a dancefloor pop-up anywhere, and Chef's Kiss is a live dance party hosted by DJ Linafornia on the first Thursday of the month in the historically Black neighborhood Leimert Park. Still, most every Sunday you can find what feels like a block party with music, food, art, and creatives selling their wares. The Leimert Park Jazz Festival began as a block party in 2015 but has become an official annual free gathering of music. In 2020 it went virtual but returned live in 2021 at the Baldwin Hills Crenshaw Plaza down the hill from where I was raised, when Baldwin Hills was considered a middle-to-upper-middle-class Black neighborhood and was referred to as the Black Beverly Hills along with the neighboring View Park-Windsor Hills, where many Black celebrities have lived and where the Duchess of Sussex grew up. Leimert Park is home to the World Stage on Degnan Boulevard,

UNITED IN REVOLT

The video shows four uniformed police officers surrounding and beating an unarmed man on the ground, using batons and tasers: these were the images that rocked the USA in 1991. The victim was Rodney King, a 25-year-old African American from Los Angeles. The police officers were later acquitted. Following the trial in April 1992 the crowd, comprised mostly of African Americans and Latinos, poured out on to the streets and clashed with the police and the National Guard. After five days of protests fifty people were dead and over a billion dollars' worth of damage had been caused. According to recent analyses the attack on Rodney King was the trigger for violence that had been held in check for decades and was turned back on to the same communities that perpetrated it. In the poorest neighbourhoods of Los Angeles, armed gangs like the Crips and the Bloods had sprung up to protect areas where the state was absent, later transforming themselves into organisations that made money from racketeering and extortion, constantly at war with each other. Their funds increased as did their weaponry, which became ever more necessary to respond to raids from the police, who countered violence with violence (47 per cent of young African Americans were gang members, according to the LAPD). And yet, in April 1992 Crips and Bloods agreed a truce, joining forces in the revolt. At the root of everything was rage at the systemic racism and daily discrimination that their fragmented and conflict-ridden communities had to face: the motive was political, even though the ruling class ignored this at the time and were more inclined to dismiss the events as the subversive acts of a crowd that had run amok.

THE PASSENGER   Lisa Teasley

Some of Everything

Pages 176–7: The Kingdom Day Parade, dedicated to Martin Luther King Jr., in 2017. The theme in 2017 was "Now more than ever, we all must work together".
Page 180: Demonstrators take part in a procession in Los Angeles on 8 June 2020 to honour George Floyd.
Page 181: Members of a marching band during the 2019 Kingdom Day Parade. The theme that year was "Healthy bodies, healthy minds, healthy democracy".

the main street, founded in 1989 by jazz drummer Billy Higgins and poet Kamau Daáood. Initially it was a collective of artists and art supporters that grew into a rich arts education space as well as a renowned performance space, hosting events on Friday and Saturday evenings.

Also on Degnan Boulevard is the Art + Practice gallery, founded by world-renowned artist Mark Bradford, philanthropist and art collector Eileen Harris Norton, and Allan DiCastro, who opened the space in 2015 and the following year went into partnership with First Place for Youth, an organization that provides transition resources for foster youth, giving them the tools for a basic foundation and stability. The former president, Bill Clinton, chose the Black-owned Eso Won Books, also on Degnan Boulevard, to host his book event; it is where I've been invited to do readings for all my own books. Eso Won opened in 1988 and in 2021 was named Bookstore of the Year by US book-trade journal *Publishers Weekly*. Brockman Gallery, the first Black-owned, artist-owned gallery in Los Angeles, was also on Degnan from 1967 to 1990 and where I first showed as a visual artist in a group exhibit.

My first solo show was at the Watts Towers Arts Center; the Towers were built

REPARATIONS

In the wake of the anger over the death of George Floyd in Minneapolis in 2020, California took a historic step by setting up a task force to work on a plan to pay reparations to the state's African-American population, in particular those descended from victims of slavery. Although the first proposal of this kind dates back as far as 1865, no compensatory measure has ever been implemented, and the Californian initiative is currently the most ambitious in the USA. The nine-member committee has discussed the various discriminatory housing policies suffered by the Black community, from property seizures to redlining, a policy of racial segregation that originated during the Great Depression with repercussions that are still felt to this day. To reinvigorate the property market at the time, 236 American cities were mapped out and divided into four zones according to the level of risk pertaining to real-estate investments: the areas coloured red – the places in which not to invest – were those inhabited by African Americans and other minorities, who consequently faced severe difficulties in obtaining mortgages and fell victim to a self-fulfilling prophecy. Recently the community of Manhattan Beach in Southern California returned the land that was unjustly seized in the 1920s to the descendants of an African-American family, but the issue of reparations is not an easy one to resolve. Who is entitled to them? In what form and to what extent? The forces opposed to this sort of policy of reconciliation have always based their arguments on the difficulties and the exorbitant costs of a broad-based campaign, and even Barack Obama described it as impractical, but the mood music seems to have changed.

by Simon Rodia (who was born in Rivotoli in the province of Campania in southern Italy) out of iron rods, spires, tiles, and cement and decorated with 7-Up cans, blue milk of magnesia bottles, and seashells. The Watts Towers is a masterpiece and pride of the city, a magnificently unique and extraordinary work of architecture that Rodia worked on from the 1920s through the 1940s. My mentor, the late, great artist John Outterbridge, ran the arts center there in the late 1980s, where children's art education in the Watts community was of primary importance. The wildly popular annual Watts Towers Day of the Drum Festival has been a steady gathering of music, drumming, and dance over the years; the last one was in September 2019, since it was not possible to stage during lockdown, still I have every hope that it will resume in 2022.

Dedicated to the exhibition of museum-quality art for the Black and Latinx communities, and with free admission, is The Underground Museum in the Arlington Heights neighborhood, founded in 2012 by artists Karon and Noah Davis. Noah died in 2015 but not without leaving a rich legacy of work that still exhibits worldwide. The museum works with cultural luminaries and artists and offers free yoga and meditation, provides fresh food, and hosts various cultural events in the Purple Garden, such as their summer series of free films and popcorn.

Most of the world sees LA primarily as the home of moviemaking, and it is certainly that, and I'm happy to see so many new Black films and television shows. The Black female friendship series *Insecure* just ended this year, 2022, with its fifth season on HBO and has been fantastic for its scenes filmed in locations all over Los Angeles, where you can see the trendy spots early thirtysomethings of all races hang out. LA comedian and director Travon Free won the Academy Award in 2021 for the short film *Two Distant Strangers*. That same year, the celebrated director Ava DuVernay, also an LA native, known for *Selma* and *A Wrinkle in Time*, was honored on Netflix and the platform showed her early documentary *This Is the Life* on the 1990s alternative hip hop scene at the Good Life Café, which was a health food market at the intersection of Crenshaw Boulevard and Exposition that became a platform for LA's independent rap scene. The famed Kendrick Lamar and Snoop Dogg are both natives, Compton and Long Beach respectively; Lamar's follow-up to his 2017 Pulitzer Prize-winning *DAMN.* and the 2018 *Black Panther* soundtrack is *KSJA*, by his group Black Hippy, which was released in 2021.

I have lived all over Los Angeles. After growing up in Baldwin Hills, I lived in Westwood while attending UCLA, then in the predominantly Jewish area at La Brea Avenue and Beverly Boulevard, in Koreatown, West Hollywood, Hancock Park, then Laurel Canyon for thirteen years in Led Zeppelin's magical party house (Laurel Canyon is known for its incredible music history), and Venice Beach for the last eight years, so I have seen the changes throughout the city up close and personal. Black people and Black culture have never been, and never could be, monolithic and ultimately cannot be defined or identified or spoken of in any one way, and, since the June 2020 protests, I have seen so many Black stars being noticed and highlighted for achieving in all areas of society—and coming from a father who worked in the all-white space program in the 1960s and who left before hitting the glass ceiling—it is a joyous thing both to witness and participate in as we lift one another and rise. ✒

THE PASSENGER   Lisa Teasley

Hollywood

on

Hollywood

I n 1886, so the story runs, Daeida Wilcox, the wife of a well-known Los Angeles real-estate entrepreneur, visited a huge plot of land on the outskirts of the city, fell in love with the place and decided to name it "Hollywood". Ignoring one small detail: there were no holly trees growing on the land. In fact, it was mainly planted with lemons and avocados. Regardless, she seemed happy to ignore this incongruity and confirmed the name because it "sounded nice". So the future capital of the film industry was established on the back of a false promise that over time became a genuine prophecy. Hollywood told a beguiling tale but one that was a far removed from any kind of reality. And in 2020, after more than 130 years during which its stories have been told all around the world, this false promise

LA MCMUSA

Translated by Alan Thawley

was caught in the glare of Tinseltown's own spotlights as never before.

It was February, and Hollywood was in celebration mode, with prizes, red carpets, trophies and acceptance speeches: the awards season was coming to an end (it normally begins in November) with the most coveted and prestigious of them all, the Golden Globes and the Academy Awards (the Oscars). In parallel, in rooms that were undoubtedly less glamourous but no less important for the world of American fiction, another institution was about to proclaim its own winner: the National Book Foundation, based in New York, which every year rewards the nation's best works of literature.

In Los Angeles, California, the old white men (if they were also troubled and nostalgic, so much the better) had already won: the film with the most nominations for the two ceremonies was *Joker*; Tarantino's latest, *Once Upon a Time in Hollywood*, was among the favourites to win best picture; and Scorsese's *The Irishman* had amassed one of the biggest hauls of prizes. Not a single woman, African-American or Latino filmmaker was up for best director at the Oscars. The list of twenty-four nominations for leading and supporting actors included just one Black performer, Cynthia Erivo, star of *Harriet*, the story of Harriet Tubman, a woman born into slavery who later became a fugitive, and her work as an abolitionist. The award for best picture ultimately went to the only non-American film in the running, *Parasite*, which was more a *unique* turn of events than a *rare* one. But the party was spoiled by a bitter aftertaste – in fact, a very bitter aftertaste – left by British comedian Ricky Gervais's opening monologue at the Golden Globes. Beneath a thin veil of irony – so thin that you might as well just brush it aside and take it at face value – he laid waste to the good intentions of Hollywood celebrities. Those who took to the stage beneath the spotlights of America's most hypocritical city and – often with an award in their hands – proclaimed their desire to fight racism and social injustice, exhorting their colleagues and the public to step up their social and political commitment to inclusivity and equality; those who spoke out about the struggle against the patriarchy, sexism and abuses of power in what studies show is still the least inclusive and least diversified of any business sector in the USA, namely the film industry: Hollywood.

"You're in no position to lecture the public about anything. You know nothing about the real world. Most of you spent less time in school than Greta Thunberg ... So if you win, come up, accept your little award, thank your agent and your god and fuck off," declared Gervais. Tom Hanks, Robert De Niro and all the rest ended up looking at the floor in a mixture of shock, embarrassment and (in some cases) a touch of indignation.

So was he right? That same month the answer seemed to come from New York, shortly before another even bigger storm – the pandemic – crashed into the bastion of untruth in the Los Angeles Hills, forcing Hollywood directly into the open jaws of Netflix. In 2020 the National Book Award went to Charles Yu's *Interior Chinatown* (Europa Editions, 2020), a novel written as a screenplay in which the author tells the story of an Asian actor working in Hollywood as a body double and an extra, who ends up being offered all the racial stereotypes constantly trotted out by the Los Angeles film world – in spite of strenuous assertions to the contrary – starting with the names he is given in the screenplays: "Generic Asian Man" or "Background Oriental Making a Weird Face".

At a time of such great cultural change in which we are now living, Mrs Wilcox's legacy seems to weigh more heavily than ever on Hollywood. It is not widely known, but if you look a little way beyond the legend and dig deeper into the geographical reasons, you'll discover that US cinema found its home in the city of Los Angeles above all because of the light: the meeting point of refracted light from the Mojave Desert and that of the Pacific Ocean creates a special atmosphere with perfect, luminous conditions. But while it is undoubtedly easier to capture a natural image under that light, it is equally the case that not everything is illuminated in the same way, starting with the city of Los Angeles itself and its inhabitants, who by rights are the main protagonists in the movies and the first to reflect the injustices of an industry that struggles to change, to become more inclusive, less racist and less sexist and therefore closer to the progressive, liberal values so often professed at its events and on its red carpets – as well as at the ballot box.

Charles Yu's novel paints a vivid, ironic picture of these contradictions, in which the content becomes the form of the writing itself. Just a few months earlier, however, another honorary citizen of Los Angeles had raged – with no hint of irony in his case – against the hypocrisy of Hollywood and its most illustrious denizens: the writer Bret Easton Ellis in his 2019 non-fiction book *White* (Knopf, USA / Picador, UK). Some of his most interesting critiques focus on the representation, both on screen and among the ranks of the showbusiness workforce, of African Americans – the people least brightly

illuminated by Hollywood's spotlights and the special Los Angeles light previously discussed.

There was a point between 2015 and 2019 when Hollywood wanted to show that it had paid its own tribute to the necessary change in attitudes: this was the period when *Moonlight* and *Green Book* won best picture (2017 and 2019 respectively), when *Black Panther* became one of the first films in cinematic history to feature a Black superhero (2018) and when two African Americans, Mahershala Ali and Viola Davis, won Oscars in their respective categories in the same year for the first time in Hollywood history (2017). Ellis charts some of these events, taking his readers to the awards evenings, to the Los Angeles parties, to the restaurants where the actors go to eat, even letting us eavesdrop on the people in the City of Angels with the power to decide which stories the world should see and which we should not. The tribute paid out in Oscars was false and hypocritical, he argues, and the situation will only change when Black people are no longer portrayed only as victims or criminals (62 per cent of gang members on screen are Black, for example), when the hero does not have to rescue his entire people from injustice, when a white man no longer needs the help of a right-hand man who is always one step behind. Even better, suggests Ellis (whose stance is much more irreverent than anti-racist), Hollywood will stop being a machine for hypocrisy and conformism when it remembers about art and what it takes to make it rather than following the morality of the day. When, rather than seeing holly trees, it acknowledges the rattlesnakes that populate its hills in far greater numbers.

An Author Recommends

A book, a film
and an album to understand
California, chosen by:

LISA TEASLEY

THE BOOK
**THE VISIONARY STATE:
A JOURNEY THROUGH CALIFORNIA'S
SPIRITUAL LANDSCAPE**
Erik Davis / Photographs
by Michael Rauner
(Chronicle Books, 2006)

At beautiful Los Angeles Echo Park Lake, there is a Latinx woman with pamphlets, preaching Jesus as savior. A white male pushes forward to take her picture then shouts with aggressive disgust, "*¡Silencio!*" I leave the brief conflict for a closer look at the lake's calming lotus blooms and see a plaque to the famed early 20th century Canadian evangelist Aimee Semple McPherson, who, in 1924, brought them from China, the flower believed to symbolize spiritual enlightenment. Stories such as the infamous and enigmatic McPherson's, legends that connect cultures, fill the pages of Erik Davis's unique book of exoteric and esoteric facts. These are the origin myths, the buildings, histories, and landscapes of my inimitably wild, explorative, and dreamlike native state, California. Although

Swami Paramahansa Yogananda filled New York's Carnegie Hall in the 1920s, he chose Los Angeles as a home for the Self-Realization Fellowship, since he considered it to be the most spiritual place in the country. He likened the city to Benares, which he called the holiest city in India. Before that, Vivekananda traveled across the US planting seeds of Vedanta, and Swami Trigunatitananda designed the landmark temple that opened in San Francisco in 1905. The Mormons also explored California during the 1850s Gold Rush years—and, outside of Utah, the Golden State has the most Mormon temples, the first one happening to be a landmark in front of my junior high school in the Los Angeles neighborhood of Westwood, where my alma mater UCLA is also located. Michael Rauner's gorgeous photographs illustrate the vast range of Erik Davis's explorations, from Neopaganism, UFO cults, and Zen boot camps to Druid Heights in the famed aquatic suburb of Marin County, populated by higher consciousness explorers such as Alan Watts, Tom Robbins, and Neil Young. All of this informs the psychic terrain that is California, and Davis and Rauner capture it exceptionally.

THE FILM
HAROLD AND MAUDE
Hal Ashby (1971)

THE ALBUM
ODELAY (DELUXE EDITION)
Beck (2008)

Although Reinaldo Marcus Green's 2021 film *King Richard* shows the huge divide between Black South Los Angeles and the white country club circuit that Venus and Serena Williams had to cross to become two of the all-time great tennis champions, and Stacy Peralta's 2001 documentary *Dogtown and Z-Boys* tells the story of the Venice Beach skateboard team and the history of skateboarding in its California birthplace, I chose to go back to the classic *Harold and Maude*, which explores the pretensions and societal, psychological, political trappings of massive wealth vs. the freedom of a creative soul who lives by her own imaginative impulses. Twenty-year-old Harold has staged fifteen suicides to get the attention of his jaded, snobbish mother when he meets 79-year-old Maude at the rain-soaked funeral of someone neither of them know. Maude's is the only yellow umbrella in a sea of black. Filmed in towns in gorgeous Northern California and in San Francisco, it is the story of a young, privileged, deadened white male's awakening to a life outside the artificial constructs of Freudian psychology, church indoctrination, and the military-industrial complex. Maude is a Holocaust survivor who lives in a train car surrounded by her art and musical instruments, and during the many hilarious adventures she takes Harold on, she points out dark ironic truths. While the 2014 film *Echo Park* (Amanda Marsalis) is an LA love story within close-up gentrification, the Academy Award winner *Crash* (Paul Haggis, 2004) connects synchronous events between races, cultures, and their interwoven prejudices, and the 1974 classic *Chinatown* (Roman Polanski) exposes the corruption on which the city of Los Angeles was built, *Harold and Maude* encompasses the broader themes of a landscape such as California.

Whenever I felt homesick during the seven years I lived in New York, I played music as classic as the Mamas & the Papas' "California Dreamin'" or as LA as the Red Hot Chili Peppers, whose lead singer I went to grade school with. And even if Golden State native Kendrick Lamar has an equally West Coast sound, I return to Beck's *Odelay* for all of its rich layers that include hip hop, bossa nova, acoustic folk, punk, country, R&B, to name just some of his influences, and these mixes, I feel, are essentially and thoroughly Californian in ways that other albums are less so in their sum total, whether it be Queens of the Stone Age, X, or any of the records Dr. Dre or Rick Rubin have produced—and Beck produces his records himself. In "Where It's At" and "Devils Haircut," Beck's voice is '90s grunge with '60s Vegas-style touches reminiscent of Jim Morrison. Beck's drums and use of samples are hip hop, and his instrumentation is folk and rock. Each song expresses more musical ideas than an entire album by most recording artists or even their career oeuvres. The irresistible rhythm of "The New Pollution," with its '60s mod whimsy, romantic sax, and ironic, even dark, lyrics offset by the upbeat sound, is something of a signature. *Odelay* was originally released in 1996 and well ahead of its time, but the 2008 Deluxe Edition includes the beautiful "Burro," sung in Spanish and featuring a mariachi band, as well as "Electric Music and the Summer People" with a Southeast Asian sitar influence that bleeds into country and blues harmonica. All of Beck's innovative songs are done with supreme understanding of sonic architecture, using garage band or punk-like distortion within a coherent structure that always surprises.

The Playlist

You can listen to this playlist on:
open.spotify.com/user/iperborea

ANTONIO DE SORTIS
Translated by Alan Thawley

If you could, wouldn't you want to be there to witness a mountain rising up out of the earth's crust or a constellation forming on the horizon, always to be present at the birth of the most amazing things? That was the promise offered by the Paramount Pictures logo, the original example of Hollywood seduction, and from then on that has pretty much summed up how we perceive the whole of the West Coast of the USA, like a perennial Big Bang, a seismic zone but also a sonic one which guarantees that, just by being there, you'll see – or hear – something new and unique as it makes its first entrance on to the stage of the world. Yet, despite its infinite number of highlights – from a memorable dawn in Death Valley to a fabulous sunset over Alcatraz – not all the protagonists of that world have sung in praise of its glorious abundance. While Otis Redding was sitting there wastin' time on his famous dock, the reasons for his long journey from Georgia to the Frisco Bay seemed to be slipping through his fingers. When in 1971 David Crosby managed to bring together the leading lights of the hippie scene, he found himself celebrating the end of the heyday of psychedelia with a self-important, doleful record. And even the Mamas & the Papas, in their most famous track, were yearning for a version of California conjured up by a winter's day fantasy. Observing the sine wave of Pacific music, with its alternating peaks and moments of relaxation, it seems that the songs on my list share a little of the spirit of those classics. Tales of legendary times, urban exoduses and tensions, written on the fringes of the Bay Area or at a Big Sur retreat by hipsters or dropouts, ecstatic or burned out. Desert guitars, muted beats, celestial loops. Californians, who are always ready to party and then immediately nostalgic because the best is already in the past, and so mature, cool or infused with kitsch that they swarm around that quintessential, impossible sound that has always been the source of everything.

1

Mazzy Star
California
2013

2

Brian
Jonestown
Massacre
Anemone
1996

3

Social
Distortion
*When the
Angels Sing*
1996

4

Tommy
Guerrero
Abierto
2003

5

Kamasi
Washington
Clair de Lune
2015

6

Frank
Ocean
Pink + White
2016

7

Foxygen
San Francisco
2013

8

Mikal Cronin
Is It Alright
2011

9

Allah-Las
Polar Onion
2019

10

Green-House
Nocturnal Bloom
2021

11

Sam Gendel
Eternal Loop
2021

12

Haim
Something to Tell You
2017

Digging Deeper

READING

Mark Arax
"A Kingdom From Dust"
The California Sunday Magazine,
January 2018

Rosecrans Baldwin
*Everything Now: Lessons From
the City-State of Los Angeles*
MCD, 2021

Chiara Barzini
Things That Happened Before the Earthquake
Doubleday, 2017

Paul Beatty
The Sellout
Farrar, Straus and Giroux, 2016
(USA) / Oneworld, 2016 (UK)

David Carle
Introduction to Fire in California
University of California Press, 2021

Elaine Castillo
America Is Not the Heart
Viking, 2018 (USA) / Atlantic, 2018 (UK)

Max Chafkin
*The Contrarian: Peter Thiel
and Silicon Valley's Pursuit of Power*
Penguin, 2021 (USA) /
Bloomsbury, 2021 (UK)

Ash Davidson
Damnation Spring
Scribner, 2021 (USA) /
Tinder Press, 2021 (UK)

Natashia Deón
The Perishing
Counterpoint, 2021

Joan Didion
Where I Was From
Knopf, 2004 (USA) /
HarperPerennial, 2004 (UK)

Conor Dougherty
*Golden Gates: The Housing Crisis
and a Reckoning for the American Dream*
Penguin, 2021

Bret Easton Ellis
White
Knopf, 2019 (USA) / Picador, 2019 (UK)

John Freeman (ed.)
Freeman's California
Grove Press, 2019

Jonathan Lethem
The Feral Detective
Ecco, 2018 (USA) / Atlantic, 2018 (UK)

Brendan C. Lindsay
*Murder State: California's Native
American Genocide, 1846–1873*
University of Nebraska Press, 2012

Alexis C. Madrigal
"American Aqueduct: The Great
California Water Saga"
The Atlantic, February 2014

Kim Stanley Robinson
The High Sierra: A Love Story
Little, Brown, 2022

David Samuels
"How Donuts Fuelled the American Dream"
1843 magazine, July 2019

Kathryn Schulz
"The Really Big One"
The New Yorker, July 2015

Anthony Veasna So
Afterparties: Stories
Ecco, 2021 (USA) / Grove Press, 2021 (UK)

Vendela Vida
We Run the Tides
Ecco, 2021 (USA) / Atlantic, 2021 (UK)

Claire Vaye Watkins
Gold Fame Citrus
Riverhead, 2015 (USA) / Riverrun, 2017 (UK)

Anna Wiener
Uncanny Valley: A Memoir (USA) / *Uncanny Valley: Seduction and Disillusionment in San Francisco's Startup Scene* (UK)
MCD, 2020 (USA) / 4th Estate, 2020 (UK)

Charles Yu
Interior Chinatown
Europa Editions, 2021

Rosanna Xia
"The California Coast Is Disappearing Under the Rising Sea. Our Choices Are Grim"
Los Angeles Times, July 2019

WATCHING

Adam DiVello
Selling Sunset
2019–

Mindy Kaling and Lang Fisher
Never Have I Ever
2020–

David E. Kelley
Big Little Lies
2017–19

Pedro Kos and Jon Shenk
Lead Me Home
2021

Marvin Lemus and Linda Yvette Chávez
Gentefied
2020–22

Lauren Morelli
Tales of the City
2019

Estevan Oriol
LA Originals
2020

Issa Rae and Larry Wilmore
Insecure
2016–21

Graphic design and art direction: Tomo Tomo and Pietro Buffa

Photography: Jana Ašenbrennerová, Ringo Chiu, Nic Coury, Josh Edelson, David Paul Morris, George Rose
Photographic content curated by Prospekt Photographers in collaboration with Josh Edelson

Illustrations: Edoardo Massa

Infographics and cartography: Pietro Buffa

Managing editor (English-language edition): Simon Smith

Thanks to: Francesco Costa, Antonio De Sortis, Alessandro Foggetta, Lauren Markham, Steve Salardino, Martina Testa, Paul Yamazaki

The opinions expressed in this publication are those of the authors and do not purport to reflect the views and opinions of the publishers.

http://europaeditions.com/thepassenger
http://europaeditions.co.uk/thepassenger
#ThePassengerMag

The Passenger – California
© Iperborea S.r.l., Milan, and Europa Editions, 2022

Translations from the Italian: Alan Thawley,
Oonagh Stransky ("Tipping the World Over"),
Deborah Wassertzug ("Decalifornication")

Translations © Iperborea S.r.l., Milan, and Europa Editions, 2022

ISBN 978-1-78770-429-9

All rights reserved. No part of this publication may be reproduced, stored in a retrieval system or transmitted in any form or by any means without the written permission of the publishers and copyright owners.

The moral rights of the authors and other copyright-holders are hereby asserted in accordance with the Copyright Designs and Patents Act 1988.

Printed on Munken Pure thanks to the support of Arctic Paper

Printed by ELCOGRAF S.p.A., Verona, Italy

Decalifornication
© Francesco Costa, 2022

Three Kids, Two Paychecks, No Home
© Brian Goldstone, 2019. First published in *The California Sunday Magazine*, November 2019.

Rematriation
© Lauren Markham, 2022

Growing Uncertainty in California's Central Valley
© Anna Wiener, 2021. First published in *The New Yorker*, September 2021.

What Does It Mean to Be a Solution?
© Vanessa Hua, 2022

Shadows in the Valley
© Francisco Cantú, 2022

Tipping the World Over
© Michele Masneri, 2022

Gone: The Burning of Paradise
© Mark Arax, 2019. Extracted from a long-form piece in *The California Sunday Magazine*, June 2019, first published under the title "Gone".

Ballot-Box Blues: The Indirect Road to Direct Democracy
© NC Hernandez, 2022

Some of Everything An Author Recommends
© Lisa Teasley, 2022

Hollywood on Hollywood
© La McMusa, 2022

The Playlist
© Antonio De Sortis, 2022

Photographs on pages 2 and 5 © George Rose. Page 2, a woman is silhouetted against the iconic Half Dome granite formation at Glacier Point, a viewing area in Yosemite National Park; page 5 shows the trunk of a giant sequoia in Mariposa Grove, Yosemite National Park.